FEEL *the* DEAL

CARMEN CAMPAGNARO

FEEL *the* DEAL

UNLOCKING SECRETS TO SUCCESS IN
REAL ESTATE AND BUSINESS

BURMAN BOOKS
MEDIA CORP.

& MEDIA

BURMAN BOOKS
MEDIA CORP.

Published 2025 by Gildan Media LLC, aka G&D Media
by arrangement with Burman Books Media Corp.
www.GandDmedia.com

Edited by Sarah Ogutu
Cover design Claire Zidar
Book design by Clarissa D'Costa

Library of Congress Cataloging-in-Publication Data is available upon request

ISBN: 978-1-7225-9916-4

10   9   8   7   6   5   4   3   2   1

CONTENTS

INTRODUCTION

YOUR DREAMS WILL BE YOUR REALITY

This book isn't just about business and real estate. It's about instinct, action, and trusting yourself when the right opportunity arises. *Feel the Deal* is about recognizing moments when numbers and intuition align—when logic meets gut instinct, and when taking the right risk can change everything.

I've never been the type to wait on the sidelines. I do my homework, I run the numbers, and I know my deals inside and out. I also trust my gut. Over the years, I've learned that the best opportunities don't always scream at you from a spreadsheet—they have to be *felt*. I can walk into a property and sense its potential before anyone else does. I've learned that those instincts, backed by knowledge, preparation, and execution, can create extraordinary results.

Real estate has been my vehicle to success, but it hasn't been a straight path. I've taken big risks; I've had wins that exceeded my wildest expectations and losses that taught me lessons no course ever could. I'm still learning, and that's what makes this business exciting.

For the first time, I'm sharing my real-life experiences. The crazy stories, the struggles, the wins, and the lessons that have shaped me. More importantly, I'm breaking down the key strategies I've used in financing, negotiation, and value creation. These aren't just theories; they're proven structures that have helped me build, scale, and sustain success in real estate.

Feel the Deal is for anyone who wants to create wealth in real estate, by developing the instincts and confidence to recognize opportunities others miss. The most successful people in this business don't just analyze deals, they *feel* when a deal is right, and have the knowledge to back it up.

What you're about to read is real. It's raw, and if you're ready to trust your gut, do your numbers, take risks, and learn from both the wins and the losses, this book could change your life.

Let's get started.

Some people *want* to succeed. They believe they're trying their best. They work harder than most, put in long hours, and hustle every day, yet, they have no idea they're sabotaging themselves. They live overly cautious lives, always preparing for the worst instead of focusing on success.

If you're one of those people, this book is for you. In fact, you *need* this book more than anyone else. The truth is, we, as humans, have the power to shape our own reality. What we focus on *expands*; if you focus on fear, you get more fear. If you focus on failure, failure follows. If you focus on what you *want*, see it, feel it; even when it looks impossible, you can make it happen. You have to believe in your success so deeply that it becomes inevitable. When life knocks you down. You get up. That's what separates those who *wish* for success from those who *live* it.

My life is a testament to this truth. I've never let circumstances, setbacks, or uncertainty dictate my path. I fix my mind on what I want and find a way to make it mine. It's like driving—your car goes where your eyes look. That's why you don't stare at the ditch. You keep your eyes on the horizon, on the sunlight illuminating the road ahead.

Today, I'm a successful entrepreneur. I'm a real estate investor, developer, builder, financier, mortgage lender, and destination vacation creator. I didn't come from wealth. I didn't always make the right choices, but I had two things that made all the difference:

First, I have *relentless* drive, determination, and energy; the most important traits an entrepreneur can have. I've never looked at an opportunity and thought, *that's too much work.* I chase the dream, I roll up my sleeves and get my hands dirty. I don't believe in the phrase, "That's above my pay grade." When people say that, I think, *Wow, you need to be humbled.*

I could retire tomorrow, spend my days lounging in a villa in the South of France, drinking and eating whatever I want. That's not me. I'd go crazy. I *need* to build, to create, to push forward. Even when I'm home, I can't just sit on the couch. I have to clean the house, bake something, or get outside in the garden.

If you have the drive to create something bigger than yourself, this book will speak to you. If you don't, but you *want* to, then get ready. You're about to see exactly what it takes.

Second, I am an *optimist.* I have a strong intuition, a positive outlook, and a highly calibrated gut. I keep my mind open to the world. I can *feel* what works and what doesn't. I'm sensitive that way, and I've used it my entire life. People say, "everything she touches turns to gold," or "she's just lucky." The truth is, it's not luck; it's intuition, experience, and the ability to trust what I *feel.*

When I walk into a building I'm considering buying, I know almost instantly whether it's right for me. Sometimes, I don't even need to step inside, I can just look at the photos and get a *vibe, this is good* or *stay away.* I always do my due diligence. I visit the property, run the numbers, and consult with my legal team. The final decision? It comes down to my gut. *Does this deal feel right?*

Every time I've gone against my gut, every time I've forced a deal that didn't feel right; it ended up being more trouble than it was worth. The transaction would drag, obstacles would pile up, and I'd have to *fight* to make it happen. In the end, it would create unnecessary stress, derail my momentum, and delay my bigger success.

When the deal *feels* right. It all comes together effortlessly. I step onto a property, look at the numbers, and I *know*, this one is mine. The deal closes smoothly. The right opportunities don't need to be forced; they align.

That has been my mantra for years: *Feel the deal.*

This book is for entrepreneurs and investors—anyone looking to build success, wealth, and a life of purpose. It's about learning to trust yourself, staying optimistic, and using both *strategy* and *intuition* to make the right moves. It's about valuing gratitude, taking action, and recognizing that success isn't just about numbers. It's about knowing when to *feel the deal* and when to let go.

You *must* understand the financials in any business deal. You need to know your business inside and out. That's non-negotiable. In this book, I'm sharing the strategies I've developed over the years that have helped me create lasting success.

This book focuses on real estate. My passion, my go-to investment, and, in my experience, the most reliable path to wealth creation.

Beyond the numbers and strategies, I want to show you something just as important: how your mindset matters.

- Be true to yourself.
- Be good to others.
- Make every business deal a *win-win* for all involved.
- See the value of the people who are part of your team.
- Never forget where you came from and those who helped you along the way.
- Work hard. Study hard. Put in the hours—*even when it feels impossible.*
- Understand that there is no get-rich-quick scheme. *Success is built, not given.*
- Stay open to the blessings waiting for you.
- Believe in the dreams you have for yourself.

The truth is, success isn't just about working harder. It's about thinking *better.* When you combine *strategy* with *belief, knowledge* with *intuition,* and *action* with *faith.* You unlock a level of success most people never reach.

To *feel the deal.*

1

THE ENTREPRENEURIAL
SPIRIT

I was just born with it—this strong entrepreneurial mindset and positive spirit. It was innately in me from the start. I first experienced mindset and manifestation when I was in Grade two. There was a White Elephant Sale at our public school in London, Ontario, Canada where I grew up. It's like a craft and bake sale. This one was held in the gymnasium of my elementary school. There was this doll, she was really tall, and super stylish. I fell in love with her. She had this cream faux leather outfit with contrast Sherpa that was green with knee-high boots and a belt, like the coolest tall walking doll ever! Her name was Wendy, I loved her so much. You had to buy a ticket to win the doll, so I asked my mom, and she gave me the money. I sat there with the ticket in hand. I looked at the doll and I repeated, "I'm going to win you." I actually saw it. I kept staring at it. All my energy was, *I am going to win this doll.* It was in my mind. No other distractions, I was focused on it. When it was time for the raffle to be called, it was my number that came up. I had no doubt I was taking Wendy home, and I did.

By Grade five, I wasn't just manifesting—I was *taking action.*

One day, my best friend since the age of three, Norval, and I were riding our bikes back from the store when we rode through Mount Pleasant Cemetery. There, in the garbage, was a massive pile of flowers, roses, carnations, beautiful arrangements that looked fresh, they were in *perfect* condition. I turned to Norval and said, "We could take those flowers and sell them." We loaded our baskets and handlebars, barely able to see the road ahead as we pedaled home. We trimmed the stems, wrapped them in newspaper, and went door to door, selling our bouquets.

Then, we knocked on the wrong door. A neighborhood florist answered. Unimpressed, she asked us where we got the flowers, and why were we selling them. She immediately asked where we lived and stormed over to my house, knocking loudly, demanding to speak to my mother. "Your daughter is selling flowers from the graveyard!" She said, outraged. My mother listened, smiled politely, and closed the door.

Manifesting isn't about just sitting around, wishing, and hoping something will happen. *You have to take action.* If you want something, or are working toward a goal—you have to put in the effort.

It all starts with mindset. Your energy, drive, positivity, and your belief all work together to shape your reality. Mindset alone isn't enough. You need to shift from *wishing* to *doing.* What steps do you need to take? What actions will move you closer to what you want?

Before anything else, you must have a strong feeling—a deep conviction that what you want is possible. You have to manifest it with your thoughts. Keep your focus sharp and your energy high. From there, action follows naturally.

That's how success works. When you see it clearly, and feel it deeply, you'll *know* when to move. When the opportunity arises, it will be obvious to take it.

My parents, Austrians by birth, immigrated to Canada in search of opportunity. My mother was *eight months pregnant with me* when she stepped onto a plane bound for Montreal. It was a bumpy ride, filled with cigarette smoke and noise, but she made the journey, determined to build a new life.

My father, Waldemar Griengl-Schott, was born and raised in Austria. He was a brilliant man, and the youngest person to graduate from his civil engineering program. His career eventually led him to Canada, where he became a senior estimator. He had a *strict* Austrian upbringing, and he raised his children the same way. He was stern, disciplined, and deeply frugal. Beneath that, he was a *warm* man, and I loved him very much.

In 2010, my father passed away from kidney disease. During his time in the hospital, I visited him every day. We talked about life, family, and everything that mattered. I was already well-established in real estate, and one day, he told me a story about our family that I had never heard before—one that made me realize that *real estate runs in my blood.*

THE GREAT DEPRESSION & A COSTLY MISTAKE

My great-great-grandfather had been heavily invested in Austrian real estate. Before the Great Depression, real estate was seen as a stable, long-term investment, especially in Europe, where land ownership had historically been the foundation of wealth and power. Property values were strong, and the belief was that owning tangible assets provided security in uncertain times.

After the Great War, with economic instability growing, my great-great-grandfather panicked. Fearing another financial collapse, he thought the smart move was to sell everything. Liquidate his real estate holdings, pay off his debts, and hold onto cash for security.

It turned out to be the *worst* decision he could have made. When the Great Depression hit, cash became nearly worthless. Inflation skyrocketed. My father told me, "People were carrying wheelbarrows full of cash just to buy a loaf of bread." The wealth that my great-great-grandfather had spent a lifetime building vanished almost overnight. Had he held onto his real estate, he would have been in a far better position to survive the economic downturn. Instead, he learned the hardest lesson in investing: panic is the enemy of long-term wealth.

REAL ESTATE AFTER THE GREAT DEPRESSION

While the stock market crashed and fortunes were lost, those who held onto real estate and hard assets were able to ride out the storm. Real estate values declined during the Depression, but they recovered, often faster and stronger than other investments. Land and property remained *real* assets that retained intrinsic value, no matter the economic climate.

The market eventually rebounded, and by the mid-twentieth century, those who had held onto their properties; or acquired them at Depression-era prices, found themselves in an incredibly strong financial position. It was a brutal, costly lesson: real estate is not just about short-term market movements; it is a generational wealth-building tool.

That lesson stuck with my father, and he passed it on to me.

THE TWO OPPOSITE MINDSETS

My father was extremely frugal. The complete opposite of my mother, Ilse, who has always loved the *finer* things in life. She is as strong and confident today at eighty years old as she was at forty. She's an Austrian beauty with blonde hair, and a smile that is both serene and mischievous. She isn't just elegant, she's *resilient*.

When she first arrived in Canada, the language barrier made her feel isolated, severing her from her natural sociability. My mother isn't the kind of woman to be held back. She found her way, like she always does.

I can see how much of who I am, comes from my parents. My father's discipline, frugality, and structured thinking. My mother's resilience, elegance, and ability to navigate anything. Most importantly, they always supported and believed in me.

I have two siblings, a brother and a sister. They are both bright and successful, my sister Regina is an interior designer and my brother Oliver is a corporate business man.

When I was three years old, my brother and I were hanging around the kitchen while my parents were cooking dinner. I reached into a box of Labatt's beer, and grabbed a bottle. Without warning, it *exploded* in my hand. I screamed. My mother rushed over, scooped me up, and placed me on the dining room table to see what was wrong. That's when she noticed a fine line across the center of my eye.

She rushed me to the hospital, desperate for help. The specialist who could treat me wasn't there, as he had stepped out for lunch. When he returned, it was too late. He had *missed the window* to save my eye.

I lost my left eye and spent months in the hospital battling an infection. My parents sued Labatt's over the defective bottle and eventually settled for $50,000, which was placed in a trust I wouldn't be able to access until my eighteenth birthday. Considering the loss of my eye, it should have been significantly more. My parents didn't speak much English and being from another country, they weren't sure of the process.

After the accident, I became a shy child. I didn't feel connected. I wasn't *me* anymore, I was the girl with the glass eye. I felt like that's *all* anyone saw when they looked at me.

I had *good* reason to feel that way. After my surgeries, I had to wear an eyepatch to school. It made me feel even more self-conscious, and the teasing was *relentless*. I was in and out of class until Grade four. I always felt like an outsider.

By Grade seven, the bullying had only gotten worse. I remember standing in line for recess one day when the boy behind me, Charlie Payne, leaned in and whispered, "Cyclops." I can still hear him saying it.

At the time, I *felt* alone. Looking back, I realized I wasn't. My family always loved and supported me. The disconnection I felt wasn't real. What *was* real was that this experience *shaped* and strengthened me.

It took years to fully embrace the fact that the things that made me *different* were also the things that made me *strong*. So much of my success in life and business has come from that strength—from learning to stand firm in who I am, no matter what challenges come my way.

When I entered high school in Grade nine, I took a different path. I skipped classes, partied with friends, and ignored my parents. I found myself drawn to the wrong crowd, following a direction that led me further away from where I was supposed to be.

By sixteen, I had dropped out of school. I got a job at Stitches, and went to live with my older sister. It was exactly what I thought I wanted—the ability to earn my own money, make my own decisions, and be independent. I *loved* it.

Even in my rebellion, I discovered something about myself—I liked working hard when I was passionate about what I was doing. I thrived on competition and quickly became one of the top salespeople in all of Southwest Ontario. More importantly, I realized that when I stayed committed to something, I could achieve whatever I wanted.

When I turned eighteen, I received the $50,000 settlement from Labatt's. It wasn't a fortune, but for an eighteen-year-old, it was enough to do something real with it. I didn't want to waste it. I went out and bought myself a Daytona Turbo Z. It was the coolest car; when I opened the door it said "the door is ajar." It was very advanced for the 1980s.

One evening, my father called me with an idea. "Why not open a video store?" He asked. It was my brother Oli's idea, he is two years younger than me but has always been business minded. It was the late '80s, and video rentals were booming. The demand was there, and Burlington, Ontario, didn't have enough stores to meet it. My father saw an opportunity. "You could work for yourself," he said. "It would be your store."

I lived in London Ontario with my sister Regina. We shared an apartment and both of us worked at Stitches. My parents moved to Burlington and I loved the idea. Not just because it was a smart business, but because it would be mine. My store.

I moved to Burlington and opened a store called My Video Store. We built it from scratch in a strip mall, every part of it, from the shelving to the signage and counters. My entire family pitched in.

We became the place to rent videos. Lines stretched out the door. I stocked a massive selection of imported candy, we sold pizza, customers could rent VCRs and Nintendo consoles, and we carried movies that other stores didn't have. The place had energy, *my* energy. It was a reflection of my pride, my vision, and my determination.

Regular customers even bought My Video Store T-shirts. I was in my flow, in my element. Two years in, to keep up with demand, we expanded into a 6,000 square foot space. My father, despite keeping his civil engineering job, helped me run the store in his free time. He worked evenings and weekends, not just because he wanted to help, but because he loved it. It allowed him to socialize, to be part of something exciting.

My father was not an entrepreneur. He was a traditional, old-school European—*be secure, get a job, pay off your mortgage, and save money.* That was his mindset, stability above all else.

I was the complete opposite. I wasn't made to work for anyone else. I didn't take direction well, and I wasn't the type to wait for someone to tell me what to do. I had to learn on my own. Jump in first, figure it out later. Sink or swim.

This is *not* always the best way to be. It cost me. It hurt me. I have the scars to prove it. That is why I am writing this so you can learn from my mistakes.

After investing in My Video Store, I still had some money left from the $50,000 settlement. I wanted to put it into something real, something that would *grow*.

I called my dad. "Let's buy a house." At first, he hesitated. Real estate was a serious commitment, and he wasn't a risk-taker. Eventually, he agreed. We bought a house in Burlington, Ontario, fixed it up ourselves, and rented it out. We did *everything*—painting, repairs, maintenance. Then we sold it, making a $100,000 profit, just before the real estate crash of the early 1990s.

It was perfect timing. Had we held onto that property even a little longer, we would have been caught in the downturn. Instead, we got out at the peak. That was the moment I became obsessed with real estate. I saw the opportunity, the ways to build wealth, the freedom it could create. This was a business I could build on. Eventually, we sold the video store, just before technology changed and the industry shifted. Another perfect exit.

That store taught me so much about business. How to sell, how to attract customers, how to make something feel alive. I may not have had a formal education, but I was street smart. I had a knack for knowing what people wanted, for seeing opportunities, and for making things work.

Then, life shifted again. I met my husband. We had two kids. I threw myself into motherhood. I was a young mother at twenty-three years old with my first born, at twenty-six I had two children. I had no problem keeping up with the demands of raising a family. I've always had too much energy. People called me the Energizer Bunny because I never stopped.

I started making clothes for my six-month-old daughter, Jordan Rain. At first, it was just hats and dresses in my basement, something fun to do with my hands. Before I knew it, it turned into a business. Soon, I had an outlet store open to the public, and I was wholesaling to boutiques across Canada.

Then, along came my son Jacob Renato. Now, I had two small kids and a business to run. Motherhood changed me. I committed my life to my babies, the most important thing in the world. I had spent my life pushing forward, building things, taking risks, and now, for the first time, I had these two little human beings who depended on me for everything. As my kids grew up, my career allowed me to take them on annual summer vacations. Touring Europe was one of the best gifts I could've given them, we made magical memories and new friends. We always toured different real estate opportunities in different countries and they would say, "mom please we don't want to see these properties." At the time it was not that fun for them.

Jordan was my first. The moment I held her, I knew my purpose in life had expanded beyond business. Motherhood transformed me. The love I feel for my babies is beyond any love I have ever felt. My kids always come first.

Jacob is my mini-me, my tall mini-me. He's 6'2" while I'm 5'2", but he is just like me in so many ways. He grew up watching me navigate real estate and business. Now he's in commercial real estate, working with such integrity and drive. He's honest, hardworking, and committed, I couldn't be prouder of the businessman he has become.

Both of my kids grew up in real estate, learning the value of hard work and seeing firsthand what it provided. I didn't just teach them about deals and numbers, I showed them resilience, discipline, and the importance of following their instincts

Jordan is my co-host on our TV show, *30 Minutes to Wealth*. Together, we've produced and edited every episode, it has been one of the greatest experiences of my life. Watching her flourish in this space, sharing knowledge and working alongside me, has been something truly special.

Jacob is out there making big moves in commercial real estate, proving that integrity and work ethic will always set you apart.

I feel so blessed to have them in my life every day, not just as my children, but as my partners in this journey. They know this business inside and out because they lived it. They grew up watching, learning, and doing.

I named my brand Bumpy Roads. It was *my* creation, *my* vision. I designed everything, the patterns, fabrics, buttons, and labels. I poured every ounce of my creative energy into it. It was the most satisfying and enjoyable work I had ever done. I *loved* being creative. I *loved* that I could build something and still have my babies around me.

By 1997, I had my best collection yet. That year, I landed an agent in New York City. One day, a sales representative approached me and said the words that made my heart race: "Neiman Marcus is interested in carrying your line." I could barely breathe. This was it. *My* moment.

That summer, a boutique that had been a regular client placed a massive order. They wanted all my inventory at the time, approximately $250,000 worth of wholesale stock. It was a *dream sale*. I had cleared out last season's merchandise, packaged it all up, and handed over the invoice with sixty day payment terms.

They came. They took the inventory. When I went to collect payment? They were gone. Stores boarded up. No forwarding address. No way to recover my money.

I had just lost everything. There was no way around it. I had to file personal bankruptcy. I learned a very hard lesson.

They say, *when one door closes, another one opens*— that is real. When you're in the middle of it, when you're standing in the wreckage of what you built, it's hard to see. Looking back, every failure, every setback, was just making room for something bigger.

One of the biggest lessons I took from that moment? Words matter. I had named my business Bumpy Roads. I thought it was a clever, endearing name. I realized I had attached my business to something that carried a *negative connotation*. It was in the name. *Bumpy Roads*. It was as if I had unknowingly invited struggle into the business from the start.

From that day forward, I made a promise to myself. I would never again name a business, company, or venture with anything less than positivity, success, and strength behind it. Words have weight.

I had to start over. This time, I was stepping into something even greater. I remember sitting in my kitchen, looking at the mess of papers in front of me. Legal documents, bank statements, invoices, all reminders of what I had lost. The weight of it pressed down on me. I had two small children, no income, and a bankruptcy to my name. Instead of feeling defeated, I felt something else, *determination*.

I picked up a pen and flipped over one of the documents. On the back, I started writing. Possibilities. Ways to rebuild.

I knew one thing for certain: If I could lose everything and still have the drive to create something new, then nothing could break me. That's when I made another promise to myself, *this time, I would build something unstoppable.*

I had no idea that real estate, my first love, was about to come back into my life in a way that would change everything.

2

GIVING OPPORTUNITIES A CHANCE

If you're an entrepreneur, you learn quickly that life will throw things at you, that you never anticipated. You will make mistakes. You will trust the wrong people. You will get bad advice. You will lose things you never thought you would.

I am not embarrassed that I had to claim bankruptcy. It was unfortunate, but when you take risks, when you put yourself out there, sometimes things don't go the way you planned. That's business.

I remember standing in my driveway, watching as someone came to take my car. It wasn't just a car, it was my only form of transportation. I stood there helpless as they hooked it up and drove away, right in front of my neighbors, and friends. I'm not sure which was worse. Losing the car itself or the feeling of embarrassment. At the same time, my marriage had fallen apart. I became a single mother, struggling to keep things together. I had no money, zero credit, and very few options.

I still remember standing at the checkout in a grocery store, realizing I didn't have enough money to pay for everything in my cart. I had to put food back. That moment stayed with me. It was humbling. It was painful. I knew one thing for sure, I was not going to stay there.

Before the bankruptcy, my father had lent me money to keep my clothing business going. My ex-husband worked as a drywaller and didn't make much, so my father stepped in to help. That money wasn't a gift, it was secured as a mortgage on my home. By then, I had a first and second mortgage equal to, if not more than, the total value of the property.

I had a small reserve to keep up with my payments, and if things got desperate, I knew I could reach out to my parents for help. That would be the last resort. I didn't want to ask for help. I had gotten myself into this, and I was determined to get myself out.

While I was in the clothing business, I met a mortgage broker who helped me secure financing for my manufacturing. Over time, he became a good friend. He saw what I had gone through and, one day, he made a suggestion that would change my life. "I think you'd do really well in the mortgage business," he said. "You should get your license."

It was a completely different industry from anything I had done before. I had the summer to take courses, and I had *nothing* to lose. So, I thought, *why not?* I was going to give it my best shot.

At the time, my son was three, my daughter was six, and I was working from my basement laundry room in our very modest side-split house. My "exquisite" desk? A fold-out table, positioned right next to the washer and dryer. I was multitasking. Running a household, feeding my kids, doing laundry, and launching a brand-new business all at the same time. That's how Pro Funds Mortgages was born.

I was sitting at my fold-out table, *busting my ass*, sending faxes to real estate agents out of a commercial investor magazine. I was determined, and *hungry*.

I took out ads in the local newspaper. "Need a mortgage? Bad credit? A difficult deal? I can help!"

I got a call from a client named Sean. He needed a mortgage for a restaurant and apartment on *the crappiest street in Hamilton, Ontario*. A restaurant mortgage, one of the hardest deals to fund. Instead of running the other way, I *lit up*.

I sent the details off to the broker I was working under at the time, and he immediately shut me down. "Don't touch this deal. It's too small and way too hard to fund."

It was a $150,000 mortgage request, nothing flashy, nothing big. I *wanted* it. I *needed* it. I told him, "No, I *can* do this. I *want* to get it done." That was it. That was my mission.

The broker said he didn't have a single lender who would touch the deal. So, I did what I do best. I picked up the phone and called every single lender, bank, and credit union in Canada.

Finally, after exhausting every option, I landed on a credit union in Manitoba. They funded the deal.

Sean was *shocked*. He couldn't believe I had pulled it off. What I didn't know, what I *couldn't* have known—was *who* Sean really was. Sean was a head speaker for the largest real estate investment training company in Canada at the time. He had an audience of 150 new students every month, all looking for ways to finance their deals.

He gave them my name. "This is the person you need to call. If you need a mortgage, *this* is who gets it done."

Suddenly, my phone was ringing. Investors were *calling me*. The real prize wasn't the $150,000 mortgage. It wasn't the small commission I made on that deal. The real prize was everything that came after.

That single moment of saying *yes* when someone else said *no*, changed the trajectory of my entire career.

Sometimes, the *hardest* deals, the *smallest* wins, are the ones that open doors you never knew existed.

Money was finally starting to come in, and for the first time in a long time, I felt like I had control again. I was moving forward.

I will never forget this one moment. I was driving up to the ATM, holding a $40,000 check in my hand. I pulled up, put the car in park, and just sat there for a second, looking at it. It wasn't just a check.

It was proof that all the late nights, all the struggles, all the times I felt like I was clawing my way out of a hole were leading somewhere. I slid the check into the machine and watched as the deposit processed. The receipt printed, and when I pulled it out and looked at my balance, I actually paused.

I have a snapshot in my mind of sitting there in my car, holding that receipt, staring at it, and just absorbing the moment. I had been at my lowest, struggling to buy groceries, having my car towed from my driveway, standing in front of the cashier, putting food back because I didn't have enough money. Now, I was sitting here, depositing a check that would have once felt impossible to make. That moment taught me something powerful. Going bankrupt wasn't the end of the world.

It had felt like the end at the time. When you're in it, when you're losing everything, it feels like you'll never come back. That's the thing about life. You get back up. You rebuild.

The first step to getting back up? Re-establishing your credit. Without a strong credit score, you won't get approved for anything, and when you're investing in real estate, your credit is everything. If you don't have good credit, you're at a disadvantage.

Your ability to borrow, to access capital, to scale a business or an investment portfolio—it all ties back to your credit. If you have good credit, you can accelerate your growth a lot faster.

If you're in financial hardship and considering bankruptcy or a formal proposal, don't rush into it. I know when you're drowning in debt, it can feel like there's no other option. Before you make that decision, see if you can negotiate with your creditors.

A lot of people don't realize this, but if you have late payments or outstanding debts, you can take it into your own hands. Call your creditors. Ask if there's a payment structure you can work out instead of immediately jumping into a bankruptcy or a consumer proposal.

Bankruptcy is extremely damaging to your credit. You don't want to go down that path over a small amount of debt that just feels overwhelming in the moment.

If you've already declared bankruptcy, if you've already had to make that tough decision, then you need to start the process of rebuilding.

The first step? Get a secured credit card. I remember the first time I heard this advice. I thought, *A secured credit card? What difference is that going to make?* The truth is, it makes all the difference.

A secured credit card is a simple but powerful tool. You put down a deposit, say $500 or $1,000, that money acts as your credit limit. It's backed by your own funds, so the bank is willing to give you a second chance. Every time you use it and pay it off, it starts rebuilding your credit history. It's not glamorous. It takes discipline, but it works. If you stay focused, if you take control of your finances and make smart moves, you can come back stronger than ever.

I went from having my car towed out of my driveway, from not having enough money to buy groceries, to sitting in my car, staring at a $40,000 deposit receipt, knowing that my life was finally changing.

The hardest moments in life aren't there to break you. They're there to shape you. They're there to push you toward something greater. I was just getting started.

If you're financially distraught, feeling like you have nothing left, and owe money to multiple creditors, there are only two options:

A consumer proposal is when a third-party bankruptcy trustee negotiates on your behalf with your creditors to create a structured payment plan. This allows you to avoid going into full bankruptcy. Each creditor agrees to an individual settlement, and you make payments based on what has been negotiated.

The problem? You still owe the money. A proposal does not wipe out your debt, it just restructures it. The worst part? A proposal stays on your credit report for seven years, just like a bankruptcy. The difference is that while you're still carrying the financial burden, your credit is taking the same hit as if you had gone bankrupt.

With bankruptcy, your debt is discharged. That means your creditors agree to wipe out what you owe, giving you a financial reset. However, a bankruptcy must be fully discharged before you can attempt to secure any new credit. Until that happens, your ability to move forward financially is extremely limited.

For me, there was no question. I was hundreds of thousands of dollars in debt. There was no restructuring or negotiating my way out of it. I had to start over. I've seen people enter into bankruptcy or proposals over $10,000 or $20,000 in debt. That's not recommended.

If you're in that situation, take control before it gets to that point. A bankruptcy or proposal will stay on your credit for seven years. That's seven years of fighting against a major negative mark on your record. Seven years of struggling to get approved for loans, mortgages, or even simple credit cards.

If you're facing this kind of decision, you need to consult an expert. The right move depends on your situation. How much debt do you have? How many creditors are involved? What are the real consequences of a proposal versus bankruptcy? Are there strategies to remove it from your credit history earlier? Is there a way to pay off your debt without having to file at all?

These are the questions people need to ask. Credit is one of the key factors in a successful real estate journey. If you want to grow, scale, and invest, you need access to credit. The way you handle financial hardship today will shape your ability to build wealth in the future.

I believe that if you're truly making your best efforts and you communicate with the person or institution you owe money to, you have a far better chance of finding a solution. It doesn't matter whether it's a private lender, a bank, or even a credit card company, the principle is the same.

If you're struggling to make a payment, don't disappear. Don't avoid the calls. Instead, pick up the phone and say, "listen, I know I'm going to be late this month, but can you give me until this date?"

Make a serious effort and communicate continuously with the party you owe. Most people, whether they are private individuals or financial institutions, will at least listen if you show initiative and a plan. If you hide, if you ignore it, if you run from it, reality is going to hit you like a brick wall. I tell anyone in that situation, just call. If you don't ask, you don't get.

Rebuilding your credit, starting over—these can be opportunities. They can be the stepping stones to something greater, but only if you take action. Call your creditors. Call an expert.

When I started over as a mortgage broker, I had no idea that the smallest deal, the one everyone else told me to ignore; would change the course of my life. It wasn't a big commission. I took a chance on it. That's what I want people to understand. When you're at your lowest, when you feel like you've lost it all, that's when you need to take chances the most. What do you have to lose?

If you lean into the opportunities hidden in the setbacks, you might find that the thing you thought was your downfall, was your greatest turning point.

3

GETTING STARTED—
BUYING REAL ESTATE

I started my new business. I started getting a taste of the success that could be obtained in real estate investing. I started to redevelop myself, learning the ropes of real estate, how rewarding it can be, and getting the bug—the real estate bug.

How can I get started in real estate with a bankruptcy, bad credit or not much money to start? The answer is complex because there are many possibilities and scenarios. First step is how are you going to get a down payment and a mortgage.

If you're at Ground Zero, you need to find somebody that can be the face for the acquisition, for the mortgage, and somebody that would assist in the down payment. There are many ways to structure a deal with less money required at closing. However the least expensive and traditional down payment is twenty-five percent with a bank mortgage. Banks and lenders make their approval decisions on what we call in the industry the three C's—Credit, Collateral, and Character. That's how a lot of lenders approve or decline a deal.

Credit is essential if you want to qualify for a traditional bank mortgage with the best interest rates. A strong credit score gives you access to lower borrowing costs, which can significantly impact your long-term success in real estate. If your credit is challenged, private lenders or alternative financing sources may still be an option, but they come at much higher interest rates.

Collateral is the security behind the loan. This means the type of property, its location, and how much equity is available. A lender will assess how secure their loan is, how easily they could recover their money if the borrower defaults. The stronger the collateral, the better the financing terms.

Character refers to the borrower themselves. Lenders want to see financial responsibility. They want a borrower with stable income, a solid job history, and a good track record of repaying debts. Even if your credit isn't perfect, your ability to demonstrate reliability and financial discipline can improve your chances of securing financing.

If your credit or financial situation is not ideal, one option is to find a guarantor. A friend or family member who is willing to guarantee the mortgage. This can be a powerful tool for getting into real estate when you don't yet have the financial standing to qualify on your own. Of course, if someone is taking on risk for you, it's only fair to compensate them in some way. A financial agreement should be structured that keeps them motivated and protected.

Regardless of how you structure your deal, it is critical to have your numbers in order. Every single cost must be accounted for, purchase price, mortgage payments, taxes, insurance, maintenance, and closing costs. When it comes time to close, there should be no surprises. You should already have a full spreadsheet of expenses so that you are ready to go when the deal comes together.

If you have the time and ability to find and structure the deal but don't have the financial means to qualify for a mortgage, then a partnership could be your best strategy. In this scenario, you act as the deal-maker while your financial partner secures the mortgage. Structuring the deal involves finding the right property, analyzing the numbers to ensure it is profitable, organizing the financing, and structuring the down payment and ownership split. In most cases, a financial partner who brings in the capital and qualifies for the mortgage would expect anywhere from fifty to ninety percent ownership of the deal. The exact split depends on the terms negotiated and the level of work you are putting into the investment.

If no financial partner is available, another strategy is to find a motivated seller willing to hold a mortgage. In this case, the seller acts as the lender, offering one hundred percent financing or holding a second mortgage while a private lender provides a first mortgage. This structure allows you to purchase with little to no money down. This scenario is not common, and if you've gone through a bankruptcy, it can be even harder to secure. However, it is not impossible. These opportunities arise more frequently in a buyer's market; when sellers are struggling to offload properties and are willing to offer creative financing solutions.

Even seasoned investors use this method to acquire properties without relying on traditional bank financing. Whenever I'm looking at a property, my first question is always: *will the seller consider holding a second mortgage?* Seller-held financing is often the most cost-effective way to borrow money. If you can secure a second mortgage from the seller, you can finance the first mortgage separately, requiring less capital to close the deal.

No matter how creative the financing, there is one rule that must never be ignored. You need a clear exit strategy.

If you don't have a plan for how to repay the loans, refinance the property, or eventually exit the deal, you could find yourself stuck in a financial bind. Every deal should be structured with the end in mind. The real money in real estate isn't just in buying properties—it's in knowing how to exit the investment profitably.

This structure can be a risky proposition if you haven't fully accounted for all the numbers and costs involved. It's easy to get caught up in finding what seems like the perfect property. One that appears to be a great deal with strong rental income that can carry a private mortgage. Without carefully running the numbers, you could find yourself in a situation where the financing isn't as solid as you thought.

Say, you find a property priced at $100,000 and secure a private mortgage for sixty-five to seventy-five percent of the purchase price. To cover the rest, the seller agrees to hold a second mortgage for thirty percent. This structure allows you to close on the deal without having to put much (or any) of your own money down, and it may even leave you with additional funds for renovations.

It is critical to understand how you will eventually pay out the private lender and transition to long-term financing with a bank. Short-term private financing is useful to get into a deal, but without a solid exit plan, you could end up stuck with high-interest debt that eats into your profits.

When I was rebuilding my financial foundation, I had to refinance a property into a bank mortgage. At that point, I asked my mother to guarantee the mortgage for me. Even though she was family, I still offered her a nominal amount for taking on that risk. She was doing something important for me, and in return, she could go out and buy something beautiful for herself.

This goes back to having trusted people in your world who believe in you enough to sign on a mortgage with you. A family member is usually the best option because they trust you more than anyone else. Finding someone to sign for you is not easy, and when people do agree, they typically want to be an owner in the property rather than just a guarantor.

If you're doing this with a friend or an investment partner, it's essential to be clear from the beginning. Everything should be in writing. You should have open discussions about ownership, refinancing, responsibilities, and how profits will be split.

It all comes down to the expectations of your partner. Some people are happy with a flat return on their investment, while others will want equity and a long-term stake in the deal.

I have had my share of nightmare partnerships. I jumped in, figured it out the hard way, and paid the price. Either I lost the property, or the partner did not contribute equally, leaving me to do all the work. Why? I didn't have a proper agreement in place. It is so important to have everything in writing.

If you don't want to hire a lawyer—although that is the best option; there are joint venture agreement templates available online. You can fill in the blanks and think about what is important to include.

Document everything, even if it sounds minor. Outline specifics on operations, compensation, exit strategies, financing, and responsibilities. Clearly define who is responsible for what and what that means in terms of ownership, workload, and profits. Most importantly, if the partner fails to hold up their end, there must be a remedy built into the agreement. A lawyer is the best person to involve, especially on the first deal.

There are so many factors to consider when buying a property, especially your first one. Where is the property located? Why is the seller selling? What is the upside potential? What renovations are needed, and how much will they cost? What are the closing costs? What will the property be worth once the work is done?

The easiest way to determine value is to ask a real estate agent for their opinion or order an appraisal. You have to do your due diligence. Real estate isn't just about buying properties. It's about acquiring stable assets that increase in value over time.

I have always compensated the people who have helped me. When I sell or refinance a deal, I make sure to compensate the partner, family member, or friend who played a role in my success. That creates goodwill. It keeps people motivated to work with you again.

Every successful business relationship I've had has been a win-win for everyone involved. I have never nickel-and-dimed my partners, trades, or anyone who contributed to my success. The more you adopt this mindset, the more good things come to you. If someone helps you, show your appreciation.

Becoming a mortgage broker gave me a deeper understanding of real estate investing and, more importantly, how to get the funding needed to make deals happen. Without financing, you cannot scale. Without access to capital, you cannot grow. Understanding how to secure funding is the foundation of success in real estate.

My first property with serious bragging rights was a waterfront home on Lake Ontario in Grimsby. It was a unique situation, one of those rare finds that felt *meant to be*. When I walked onto that property, I had that feeling. The one I get when I know it's the right one. My gut told me *this is it*. Some properties whisper, but this one screamed at me.

This is what I mean when I say, Feel the Deal. When you visit a property, how does it feel? Does it pull you in? Does it make you want to move forward no matter what? That instinct, combined with running the numbers and knowing the potential, is what separates an average deal from an extraordinary one.

I found this property in the newspaper, listed as a private sale by owner. These are my favorite kinds of deals. No real estate commissions, direct negotiation, and often, the most flexibility in structuring a purchase. The moment I saw the listing, I knew it had potential, but when I arrived and saw it in person, I was hooked.

It was a beautiful old lake house, sitting on three acres of land with massive old trees—oaks, maples, and fruit trees heavy with apples, pears, and peaches. This area was once renowned for its fruit farms. I could feel the history rooted in the land. The house itself was old but special. Originally a single-family estate, it had been converted into a triplex, with three separate rental units. The potential for cash flow was strong, and the property itself was priceless.

One of my favorite moments in real estate is the first walkthrough after closing. When the deal is done, the property is mine, and I finally get to explore every inch of it. As soon as I stepped inside, I felt drawn to the basement. It was packed with random old things. Nothing too exciting at first. Then, tucked away in a dark corner of a fruit cellar, I found an old safe. My heart raced as I opened it, half expecting it to be empty. Inside were old documents dating back to the early 1700s. Original land deeds detailing the history of Grimsby itself. These papers recorded how the land had been divided and sold over the centuries, including who owned it and for how much.

Holding those documents in my hands, I felt a deep connection to the history of the place. It wasn't just a real estate deal anymore, it was a piece of the past. I knew immediately that I would frame these documents and keep them in my office as a reminder of where I started.

I also discovered a stunning old vase, tucked away in a forgotten corner of the house. It turned out to be very valuable, but I've never sold it. It sits in my office to this day, a constant reminder of one of my first big real estate buys, a symbol of trusting my instinct and going after what I knew was a great deal. This property was more than just an investment, it was validation that I could see opportunities where others didn't.

I met with the seller. Whenever I negotiate a deal, my first strategy is to ask the seller to hold a mortgage. A second mortgage is always my first ask because it allows the seller to receive a portion of the money upfront while deferring taxes on the remaining amount until the funds are paid back. It's a win-win if structured properly. He was asking $450,000, and since this was a private sale with no real estate commissions involved, I knew I had room to work with.

"I'll give you close to what you're asking, and I can close quickly," I told him. "I'm planning to renovate and increase the value of the house, but I'll need you to hold a second mortgage. I'll secure a private first mortgage and disclose everything to the lender so that the entire deal is above board. No hiding anything."

Most banks won't allow a second mortgage when the total loan amount exceeds the purchase price, but private lenders are more flexible when everything is transparent. To my excitement, he was open to it. This deal was happening!

This type of structure isn't cheap. I was securing more financing than the purchase price and putting none of my own money into the deal. Yes, this is a reality, it happens more often than people think!

Being in the mortgage business gave me an edge. I had the relationships and knowledge to secure a private first mortgage quickly, we were able to close in less than thirty days.

Before finalizing everything, I ordered an appraisal and a building condition report to ensure there were no surprises. The private lender was aware of the second mortgage, and I ended up securing about 110 percent of the purchase price. If I paid $450,000, I was getting around $500,000 in funding. That extra money gave me what I needed to close the deal and begin renovations.

This property had three rental units, and the rents were strong. They covered the payments on both the first and second mortgages, meaning the property essentially paid for itself every month. It wasn't heavily cash-flowing, and I knew I had a better opportunity elsewhere.

After one year, I decided to sell. I didn't list it on the market. Instead, I placed an ad in a local magazine and found a private buyer directly. The deal closed with a $150,000 profit. That moment changed everything for me. The deal had been creative, structured outside of traditional financing, and executed quickly.

I moved on to my second opportunity, a four-unit property in Burlington, Ontario, once again on the lake. This property stood out to me just as much as the first—historical, beautiful, and filled with character. There's something about these older homes that I've always been drawn to, not just because of their architecture but because of the history they carry. Just like with my first property, I found some incredible treasures inside.

At that time, financing options were far more flexible than they are today. You could get ninety-five percent financing with an insured mortgage, on top of that, I was able to secure a construction renovation loan for $40,000. I was still dealing with the bankruptcy on my credit report and couldn't qualify for a bank mortgage, so I asked my mom to co-sign with me. With her name on the mortgage, we secured the ninety-five percent financing plus the additional $40,000 needed for renovations.

I purchased the house for $450,000 and estimated that I needed an additional $30,000 to complete the renovations. In a typical scenario, this would have required a $27,500 down payment, but because of the way financing worked at the time, the bank advanced close to the purchase price.

Back in 2005, it was incredible. Banks were offering cash-back incentives at closing. The trade-off was a slightly higher interest rate, but they would give back five percent of the loan amount as cash, which could be used for the down payment. That was exactly what I did. It was a very creative structure.

Once again, I renovated the home and held onto it for a couple of years. It was fully rented, and the property cash flowed. The rents covered all expenses, and I was building equity with every passing month. Eventually, I decided to sell, walking away with a great profit.

This strategy of buying, renovating, and selling for a lift became a stepping stone. It was the perfect way to build capital and move into larger deals. At the time, I was using real estate to generate down payments that I simply didn't have when I first started. If I could go back in time, I would have kept the properties. That $450,000 property is now, twenty years later, worth over $3 million dollars.

Real estate is a powerful tool for leverage. It allows you to borrow against your assets when needed, and if you hold onto properties long enough, the wealth accumulation is unmatched.

The third opportunity came right after. It's interesting because deals always seem to come to me in threes. This was the third Lakeshore address I had acquired within twelve months. It was another creative financing deal.

At the time, I was still working out of my basement, but my business was growing rapidly, and I desperately needed an office space. This property was perfect. It was an old, four-level house on Lakeshore Road, full of charm and history. I put in the offer with a plan to renovate the lower level to create additional space.

For this deal, I used my father's credit. Once again, we secured ninety-five percent financing, and this time, I was in a much stronger position financially. My business had taken off, so I was able to personally cover the down payment and closing costs.

This investment was different from the others because I wasn't just buying it to rent or sell. I was buying it for my business. I moved my offices into the property, I converted the lower level into a one-bedroom apartment. It was a wise decision, as the rental income from the tenant covered the majority of my mortgage payments. This became my office for several years.

Those were the three properties I bought in one year. All three of them were right for me, I Felt The Deal. I went to see the properties and I knew immediately they were the right choice and meant for me. It happened very naturally. It came together. It felt right. Most of the deals I've done in my life have been with little or no money of my own. it is all about the creative structure.

People should stay in their comfort zone, which allows you to sleep at night. You don't have to go into the market buying everything. Start small. Make your contacts and build your relationships. Find just one good property. Learn and do only what you can handle in your life. Make decisions one step at a time. You can't build on a shaky foundation.

You don't have to dive into the market buying everything in sight. Start small. Take the time to build your contacts and relationships. Find one good property. Understand it inside and out. The biggest mistake people make is overextending themselves too soon.

Real estate is not a sprint, it's a long game. The people who succeed are the ones who take the right steps at the right time. When the right deal comes along, you'll feel it.

4

BUILDING YOUR
REAL ESTATE BUSINESS 101

If you're going to build your real estate business, you have to have a strong foundation. As you grow it will need to be stable and reliable.

YOUR FUNDING, YOUR FINANCIER, YOUR BUYING POWER!

Before you start looking for the property, the most important thing is access to capital. Be it a mortgage, line of credit, cash or a partner. You need to come in with money, be able to qualify for a mortgage or pay cash. Putting together a financial package and meeting with your financier would be a wise first step. A net worth and income statements are the first items required to have an indication of what type of property you could qualify for. For example, if you have a single-family home and a rental property. What is the mortgage? How much do you pay for your property taxes? Is there any income derived? Your financial package is the big picture of who you are, your experience and what you've done. As a mortgage broker, when I pick up a deal, there's a list of questions I ask and I can tell you shortly thereafter what you could probably qualify for.

We are back to the three Cs. Credit, Collateral, and Character. It's what institutions, B type lenders or private money lenders typically look at. Why are you borrowing? What's your credit score and income like? What type of property are you financing? Where is the property located? What's your ability to repay, what is the exit?

It would be wise to put together all your documents, tax returns, your notice of assessments, your net worth, your mortgage statements, and your leases. You need to have everything that has to do with your financial situation. So when you're ready to go for financing, you can open the file and move forward. Keeping this up to date will always focus you on where you are. A mortgage broker assessing your file, will be grateful for your organization.

So many people do not realize how tarnishing it is to shop around for a mortgage. It's really important to build loyalty with your team. Find the people you really want to work with. Find a broker that you feel confident with, that can assess your package, provide you with a definite direction and a pre qualification. It is important that you have a relationship with the mortgage broker. Be fully transparent so they know everything about you. If you hold back information, the broker handling your file will not be able to make the appropriate assessment and this could jeopardize your financing.

Going to multiple parties, *shopping for a deal* is not good. I remember many years ago an investor, secured a really great deal, he went in firm, with no conditions. That was his own doing, however he felt confident that he could get the financing. I was working with him and I felt confident that I could get him the financing as well, but little did I know that he went to three other institutions and another mortgage broker. I sent it to one institution and it had come back in that another mortgage broker had sent it into the same institution. That mortgage broker lied on the application. It was inconsistent. The bank declined, flagged it, and this investor was flagged in the system as fraudulent. The investor could not secure the mortgage with a bank as he could have prior to shopping. We did secure private capital for him however at double the cost. Work with one person, someone that you're comfortable with, that you have faith in, a mortgage broker for investment properties, and then that person can facilitate almost everything that you need as you grow.

Just for perspective, I had been working very hard for one of my clients and received the approval with excellent terms. I receive a call and he says "Oh, I'm going with this other mortgage broker." I was really upset, to put it mildly. That's not loyalty, and it's not honest. Then the investor client comes back to me and says, "Oh, that didn't work out. Can you get me that mortgage again?" I told him that I'll do it, but expect no favors.

When you are loyal to whomever you're working with, you build trust, and when you are in need of a favor, a quick closing, a bridge loan, a reference, or a letter of approval, the person working for you will vouch for you. It will take you much further ahead.

THE NEXT PERSON YOU WANT ON YOUR TEAM: A LAWYER

If you're serious about growing in real estate, the next person you want on your team is a lawyer. Not just any lawyer, a damn good one.

Finding the right fit might take some time, and as you scale, you'll need different lawyers for different tasks. The best way to start? Referrals. The right lawyer won't just help you close deals—they'll help you grow your business.

You don't need just any real estate lawyer. You need someone who does more than just close residential deals. You want a lawyer who knows how to close private money transactions, structure commercial deals, and navigate planning and development. More importantly, you need a lawyer who is business-minded. They should be able to set up your corporations, draft bulletproof joint venture agreements, and, most critically, be a top-tier negotiator.

Some lawyers just want to "lawyer up." They feel the need to prove they're the smartest person in the room, they kill deals instead of making them happen. These lawyers are deal breakers, not deal makers.

What should you look for? Sharp, clever, charismatic, a super negotiator, someone who doesn't just tell you what can't be done but finds ways to always make it happen.

Over the years, after closing billions in transactions, I've learned that having the right lawyer in your corner can make or break your deals, not to mention save you a lot of money. They're the ones at the finish line when you need a last-minute extension. Want to negotiate a credit on closing, and much more complicated issues when you get into larger deals? Your lawyer is the one who either pulls it off or lets it fall apart.

I have a lawyer I work with Rocky, he is so expensive. When I think about how much he's saved me on deals, it pays for itself. I just hope he never reads this, he might start charging me even more.

Here's how I found him: I was working on a closing, and he was representing the seller of a property we were buying. He was brutal, only because I was on the other side. I remember thinking, *Wow, this guy is not fun to deal with. If he's this tough against me, I need him on my team!* That's exactly what I did. I aligned myself with him immediately.

So many people in business stress over the nickels and dimes instead of focusing on the big picture and what's ultimately going to get them ahead. You have to run a tight ship; watch your expenses, and be prudent. My philosophy has always been simple: everyone needs to be paid, everyone needs to win.

THE NEXT KEY PLAYER: REAL ESTATE AGENTS

If you're investing in your own backyard, I highly recommend working with one real estate agent you trust, and most importantly, being loyal to them.

Loyalty creates opportunities. When an off-market deal comes up, your agent will think of you first. They might say, "I have a deal for you. It's not listed on MLS. I want to give you the first shot because I know you close deals and you're loyal."

That's how real estate works, relationships matter. It's about having ethics, integrity, and treating people the way you want to be treated. Too many people disrespect others' time, making everything about themselves. The best deals happen when everyone wins.

INVESTING OUTSIDE YOUR BACKYARD

If you're looking in a market where you don't know anyone locally, I've had great success by contacting the listing agent directly.

- You don't always know how close they are to the seller.
- They represent the seller, now they'd be representing you, too.
- Their loyalty might not be 100 percent neutral.

- They're motivated to deal with you directly because they earn a bigger commission.
- The seller saves money by only paying one agent.

THE RISKS OF DEALING DIRECTLY WITH A LISTING AGENT

Money motivates people. That can be both good and bad.

For example, if the listing agent is best friends with the seller, they might subtly steer the deal in the seller's favor. Even with required disclosures, they may slip in contract clauses that don't work in your best interest. If you're new to the business, you might not catch these details.

My advice? Always have your lawyer take a quick peek at the contract. Just tell them, "Please be nice on the fees, this deal isn't 100 percent locked in yet."

Real estate agents are highly regulated. I've seen first-hand that in smaller communities, some agents don't care about the rules as much as they should. So always stay sharp, protect yourself, and build relationships with trustworthy professionals.

A PERSONAL EXPERIENCE:
HOW I LANDED MY DREAM PROPERTY

I had an opportunity to rent a cottage with my kids and mother, the location was on Lake Huron in the most beautiful and natural place I had been. The area is true northern Ontario with sandy shallow beaches combined with the traditional northern landscape. The lady renting the house had a rent to own arrangement for a very appealing price. After the visit I had asked the lady if she ever sells, to let me know. That fall she called and told me I could have the property for she what she paid, $100,000 as long as she could stay for twelve months in the back apartment. SOLD! Since then I slowly built myself in the community, where my kids were able to make memories of our amazing summer getaways.

I started buying real estate in a very small, tight-knit community. A stunning area where most residents were seasonal and properties were passed down through generations. Rarely did a prime property hit the open market. When it did, it was usually sold to a family member or a close friend before anyone else even got a chance.

This story is particularly interesting. It involves a property I had my sights on for over twenty years. I wanted it so badly that I left letters in their mailbox multiple times over the years, hoping that when they were ready to sell, they'd consider me.

One day, I got the call. A trusted Realtor I had worked with for years, Mrs. Deal one of the best Realtors I have worked with, someone who had seen my loyalty and ability to close deals, reached out to me. She told me this exact property was now listed for sale.

THE VALUE OF LOYALTY IN BUSINESS

Let me take a quick detour. I earned this Realtor's respect by paying her a commission even on a deal that ultimately went through privately. By contract, I didn't have to. I did it anyway because I believe in long-term relationships over short-term savings.

A COMMUNITY THAT DIDN'T WANT ME

I was beyond excited and told my Realtor, "I NEED to get this one."

There was a problem. Even though I had been investing in the area, the locals didn't like me. They had heard about me—this person coming in, buying, renovating, and renting short-term properties. They did not like change and, they did not like me.

I would go to a garage sale and hear people talking about me. The person in control of the estate, the trustee managing the sale, told my Realtor: "I don't want that Carmen person to buy this property."

HOW I GOT THE DEAL ANYWAY

The property was listed for $1,250,000, and there were multiple interested buyers. I wanted it more than anyone else. I wrote a letter to the trustee, the person making the decision. I asked, "Why don't you like me? What have I done?"

I told her about my family, my vision, and my love for the property. I asked her to reconsider and allow me the opportunity to buy it. To show how serious I was, I made an offer:

- $1,350,000—$100,000 over asking
- Thirty day closing
- No conditions

I thought this would make it an easy decision.

Just in case, I arranged for a second offer through another party. One that would later assign the contract to me.

- This offer was $50,000 below asking
- Thirty day closing
- No conditions

This meant that if she accepted my offer, the beneficiaries would receive $150,000 more than the other offer on the table. Despite this, the trustee refused to deal with me. Even though she was responsible for handling the sale on behalf of ten beneficiaries, she still chose the other offer, costing them all $150,000.

THE WIN

In the end, I closed on the deal anyway. I saved myself $150,000. This was one of my best acquisitions ever.

It came with:

- Four waterfront lots
- A fully furnished vintage home filled with treasures
- An overall value of $2.5 million, with each lot alone worth over $500,000

This experience taught me a lot about perception, persistence, and the power of relationships. At the end of the day, people may not like you, but business is business. If you're strategic, loyal, and relentless, you'll find a way to make the deal happen.

THE DEAL THEY DIDN'T WANT ME TO HAVE

This deal taught me a valuable lesson: emotions and biases often get in the way of good business decisions. The trustee was so focused on not selling to me that she left $150,000 on the table.

Here's the irony: her refusal ended up working in my favor. I got the property anyway, and for less than I was willing to pay. A prime waterfront estate with a total value of $2.5 million. Persistence and strategy win over personal opinions, I got it anyway.

PROPERTY MANAGEMENT: YOUR GREATEST ASSET OR YOUR BIGGEST RISK

If there is one thing I have learned in this business, it is that property management is everything. You can have the most beautifully designed buildings, the best locations, and an impressive portfolio. If your management is weak, your entire operation can fall apart faster than you ever imagined.

I strongly believe that when you start in real estate, you should manage your own properties. I say this because I have seen people hand over control of their investments too soon, putting their trust in property managers who were either incompetent or outright dishonest.

WHY YOU NEED TO MANAGE YOUR FIRST PROPERTIES YOURSELF

For the first few years, I believe every investor should manage their own properties. You need to experience it, to get a feel for what it really takes to run a successful rental business. You should know when and how rents come in. You should understand what it takes to keep a property running smoothly. You should be aware of where money is being spent.

There are so many hidden costs in property management, and if you are not paying attention, they will add up fast. Some of the expenses you need to be familiar with include snow removal, garbage collection, cleaning and maintenance of hallways and common areas. Unexpected repairs, everything from plumbing emergencies to heating failures in the middle of winter.

Once you have learned the ins and outs of how a property should be managed, only then should you consider hiring a property management company. Even then, you must ensure that you fully understand the process so that you are not left blindly trusting someone else to handle your assets.

THE HARDEST LESSON: WHY I WILL NEVER USE A THIRD-PARTY PROPERTY MANAGER AGAIN

I wish I could tell you that I learned this lesson early and avoided disaster. The truth is, I learned the hard way, and it cost me millions. If I had a book like this when I started in real estate, I would have saved a fortune, and years of setbacks.

The only book I ever read back then was Rich Dad, Poor Dad, and while it gave me the push I needed to get started, it did not teach me how to protect myself from being scammed in property management. That is why my company manages all of our own properties.

HOW I GOT BURNED

One day, a well-connected Realtor, let's call him Mr. Teflon, came to me with a golden opportunity. It was a forty-nine unit townhouse complex that was legally structured as a condominium, but it was operating as an apartment building.

The plan was simple. Buy all forty-nine units in bulk, then sell them to investors individually for a profit margin. Investors would renovate the units and either resell or rent them out, with a huge upside for everyone involved.

On paper, it looked like the perfect deal. Then Mr. Teflon introduced me to a property manager who was supposed to be a superstar Mrs. Angel. She assured me she had everything under control, telling me, "I'll take care of everything. You can put all the trust money in this account. I have my own trades, and I'll get the work rolling." She seemed incredible. She showed up at my office every other day, always working hard.

Then, everything fell apart. One day, I looked at my accounts and saw that all of the investor renovation money was missing. She had been intermingling funds, shifting money between projects she was running. Ultimately, she took off with millions of dollars. She fled the country. Flew to South Africa. Bought herself a house on the ocean. Just to rub it in, she sent me a picture of her standing in front of it.

Meanwhile, I was left with a financial and legal disaster. Investors thought I had stolen their money. It took me three years to clean up the mess.

She wasn't just targeting me—doctors, lawyers, and other investors got scammed too. The documents had been manipulated, appraisals, building condition reports, critical due diligence documents. This was a multi-million-dollar deal, it was an absolute nightmare to unravel.

I lost millions. I had to sell my new office, move to a tiny rental space, and cut my staff down to two people just to survive. I almost lost everything.

Funny enough, this is how I met my husband, Rambo, the best thing that happened to me. He was in property management at the time and came in to help clean up the mess. He saw firsthand how bad it was. None of the renovations were done. The money was gone. The paperwork vanished. That's when I made a permanent decision: I will NEVER trust a third-party property manager again.

WHAT YOU MUST DO TO PROTECT YOURSELF

If you are going to hire a third-party property manager, follow these non-negotiable rules.

Make sure they are bondable, meaning they have legal accountability for handling client funds. Get referrals from people you trust, and don't just take their word for it. Verify their reputation. Experience matters.

Go to real estate investment networking events, ask around, and see if anyone has worked with them before. Visit their office and see if it is clean, professional, and well-organized. If it is a mess, with papers everywhere and chaos, that is a red flag.

Manage your own money. Rents should always go to your account first, and the property manager should get paid from you, not the other way around.

THE SCAM THAT NEARLY TOOK EVERYTHING

I thought I was making a smart business move, leveraging my reputation, working with trusted investors, and relying on a property manager who seemed like a superstar. Instead, I learned one of the most painful lessons of my career: never let someone else control your money.

THE TRADES: YOUR BIGGEST ASSET OR YOUR WORST ENEMY

The project in Florida was a dream, eight beachfront houses directly on the soft, sugar-white sands of Fort Myers Beach. These weren't just ordinary houses—they were handpicked, purchased with a vision, and destined to be transformed into luxury short-term vacation rentals.

For me, perfection is the standard. Every single detail—from the design to the cleanliness to the guest experience, had to be flawless. That is what separates an average rental from a must-visit destination.

Fort Myers Beach had everything I was looking for. When we purchased these properties in 2019, I knew this was an area with serious upside. I had already been active in the Naples area for over five years. I wasn't lounging by the pool or sipping cocktails on the beach. That's just not me. I was in my car, driving up and down the coast, studying the landscape, observing neighborhoods, and analyzing where the best opportunities lay. That's how I found Fort Myers Beach.

From Marco Island to Sarasota, almost everything had already been developed, modernized, and upgraded. Except for Fort Myers Beach. It had a quirky, old Florida charm, but it lacked high-end, professionally managed vacation homes, the kind that I knew would be in huge demand.

Then I met Mr. King. Everyone calls him the King of Fort Myers Beach, and he lives up to the name. He knows every deal, every property owner, and every opportunity before it even hits the market.

He started bringing me properties, beachfront homes, side by side, directly on the water. A compound of luxury beach houses, designed to create an unforgettable rental experience.

They needed a lot of love. They were dated, worn down, and neglected, but that never scared me. I loved the challenge. We rebuilt everything, from the ground up. When they were completed, they were stunning.

We rebranded the properties as Sugar Beach Homes on Fort Myers Beach, and they became a major success. The interiors were bright, beachy, and inviting, with carefully selected details that made every space feel unique. The exteriors were picture-perfect, combining luxury with the laid-back, sun-soaked vibe that travelers craved.

Just when everything was finally perfect, Hurricane Ian hit.

The news came in, tracking the storm as it formed over the ocean, slowly making its way toward Florida. At first, we were not overly concerned. We had been through storms before. We assumed there would be some damage, but nothing we could not fix quickly. We had just finished major renovations on all eight homes. Everything had been rebuilt. The decks, the staircases, the landscaping. Every last detail was perfect, ready for the busiest rental season yet.

Then Ian made landfall. The damage was unlike anything I had ever seen before. The entire island was washed away. The water surge was over twelve feet high, and the destruction was absolute. It looked like something from a movie. Entire homes had vanished. Boats were sitting where houses once stood. Roads were unrecognizable, covered in debris, flooded beyond belief, the town looked like a war zone.

When the storm passed, I finally received confirmation of what I feared. Three of our eight homes had been completely destroyed. The other five were unrecognizable. The damage was so severe that only two of them were even salvageable. Everything we had just completed, all of it, was gone. We had investors who needed answers. We had an entire business to rebuild. We had insurance claims to process, work to start, and a ticking clock before the next season.

Fort Myers was never sleepy. It was a hidden gem. The community was ripe for redevelopment after being hit with a hurricane more devastating than they had seen in over a hundred years, due to the rare bend along the coast.

That was when Mr. Scam stepped in. He had been our contractor for the deck and staircase work before the storm. He had done all eight properties, and his work had been solid. He had a good track record with us, and I had no reason to question him. He had done great work before, and I trusted him.

When the storm cleared, he called me immediately. "I will make sure your properties are my first priority after the storm." I was relieved. I needed someone who knew the properties inside and out, someone who could get things moving as fast as possible. He had a history with us, that gave me confidence; but I had a bad feeling. Something about his urgency, the way he kept talking about the money first, before even discussing the full scope of work, made me uneasy. I ignored it.

A substantial deposit was sent to him, so that work could begin immediately. It was not my mistake, nor was it a lack of oversight on my part. The contractor had gained my trust through prior work. His deception was not something I could have foreseen at the time. Then he asked for more. He needed another deposit. Before I knew it, we had paid him four hundred and fifty thousand dollars, and barely anything had been done.

I sent one of my team members down to Florida from Canada to check on the work. That was when we realized we had been completely scammed. Mr. Scam had barely started anything, I believe he renovated his own house with our money!

Then we uncovered the worst part. He was not even licensed in the state of Florida. In Florida, operating as an unlicensed contractor is a felony, and people go to jail for it.

Sometimes, in business, the biggest mistakes happen when we convince ourselves to ignore our instincts. If something feels wrong, it usually is.

I have learned that in real estate, you can recover from bad deals, and you can rebuild lost money, but you cannot afford to ignore your gut instinct. Some people simply take advantage of trust, and no amount of preparation can always protect you from that.

The devastation of Hurricane Ian will never be forgotten, but what followed has been one of the biggest transformations in the history of Fort Myers Beach. What was once a sleepy, underdeveloped beach town is now on the radar of global developers. Five-star hotels are purchasing oceanfront land. Major developers from around the world have their sights set on Fort Myers Beach, seeing what I saw years ago, the incredible potential of this location. The land values doubled and In a strange way, Ian created a real estate gold rush. I saw the value in Fort Myers Beach before the storm.

One of the most important relationships you will ever build in real estate is with the trades. It is one thing to find people who can do the job well. It is an entirely different challenge to find people who are honest, reliable. If there is any part of this business where people will try to take advantage of you, it is in construction. This is why we decided to run our own construction company.

Time and time again, I have put my trust in contractors, believing their promises, only to be blindsided by dishonesty, shortcuts, or outright fraud. I have seen it all, projects left unfinished, budgets mysteriously inflated, payments disappearing without a trace. It has happened so often that I wish I could say experience alone makes you immune to it. Even after seeing every trick in the book I have still found myself in situations where I trusted the wrong people.

FUNDING: THE POWER OF CREATIVE FINANCING

I have structured many of my deals using 100 percent financing, leveraging other real estate assets and Vendor Take Back (VTB) financing. This is one of my trade secrets. A strategy I've used successfully for both myself and my clients over the years.

Let's say you own another property, and there is equity available, meaning the difference between the mortgage balance and the property's market value gives you some borrowing room. If you have twenty-five to fifty percent equity, you have options to pull funds and reinvest into a new deal without using cash out of pocket.

A VTB works best in a challenged market, when sellers are highly motivated and need to sell quickly. In these cases, they may be open to holding a mortgage on the property as an incentive to get the deal done. A VTB can be structured as either a first or second mortgage, where the seller agrees to finance a portion of the purchase price rather than requiring the buyer to come up with the full down payment in cash.

The best strategy is to ask the seller to hold the VTB in second position, as getting a first mortgage is easier. The first mortgage is often secured through a traditional lender or private financing, while the second mortgage, the portion usually covered by a down payment, is funded by the seller.

A VTB is an excellent tool for both new and experienced investors. I use them all the time. Let's look at a simple example:

Say you're buying a duplex and you need a mortgage. A traditional lender will typically finance seventy-five percent to eighty percent loan-to-value. Where do you get the remaining twenty to twenty-five percent?

Even if you have the down payment sitting in your bank account, do you really want to use it all on one property? Some investors prefer to grow slowly and take a more conservative approach, which is fine. For those looking to scale faster, using all your cash on one deal is not always the smartest move.

A VTB allows you to spread your capital further. If a bank is willing to give you seventy-five to eighty percent financing, you can negotiate a ten to twenty percent VTB with the seller, often at a much lower interest rate than private financing.

Instead of securing the down payment with a private lender at fifteen percent interest, you offer the seller five percent interest on the VTB, which makes the financing far more cost-effective.

Here's where it gets tricky. Most institutional lenders do not allow VTBs because they want buyers to have their own funds invested in the deal. However, there are B-lenders and alternative financing sources that do allow VTBs, and a good mortgage broker can find them for you.

One of my favorite creative strategies is to secure the VTB on another property instead of the one being purchased, Instead of registering the second mortgage (VTB) on the new property, you register it against a different property you already own. This allows you to:

1. Bypass restrictions from lenders who don't allow VTBs on the subject property.
2. Use the VTB as a recognized mortgage commitment, which helps when showing the lender that you have the required funds.

Banks usually want to see the down payment sitting in your account for a minimum of ninety days. If you don't have liquid cash, this strategy allows you to document the borrowed funds as a secured mortgage commitment, making it acceptable to the lender.

This is an extremely effective strategy when structured correctly, as it allows you to:

- Secure 100 percent financing on a deal.
- Preserve your own cash for future investments.
- Obtain better financing terms by structuring the second mortgage at a lower interest rate.

If you can find a seller willing to hold a VTB, and you have equity in another property, this is an incredible way to leverage your assets and grow your portfolio without using your own money.

A VTB is beneficial to the seller because it allows them to defer capital gains tax on the portion of the sale price that they finance. Instead of paying a lump sum in taxes the year they sell, they only pay tax on the amounts they receive each year as the buyer repays the loan. This tax deferral can make a VTB an attractive option for a seller, especially in a buyer's market or when they want to earn steady interest income on their money.

For the buyer, a VTB can be game-changing. If the seller is willing, they may even lend more than the purchase price, as much as 120 percent of the purchase price.

With the additional financing, you close the deal with no money down, complete renovations, and rent out the property to stabilize it. Once the renovations are done and the property is fully rented, you refinance with a bank at a lower interest rate, and you now have a fully stabilized asset that you acquired with none of your own money.

The key to success is understanding the terms of the mortgage. The structure of the deal must be strategic. If it takes one year to renovate, lease up, and increase the value of the property, then you should secure a one-year term with the seller and any lenders involved.

At the end of that twelve month period, you refinance, pay off the seller's loan, and move forward.

Sometimes, paying off the VTB isn't the best move. If the seller's VTB is at five percent interest, why rush to pay it off? If the deal still cash flows with that financing in place, you may be better off keeping it and using your capital for your next investment. This is a great way to scale faster.

This approach isn't for everyone. Time and energy are critical factors. If you have a full-time job, a family, and other commitments, aggressively scaling your portfolio this way might not be realistic. Real estate investing requires focus, effort, and strategic planning. Some people can handle rapid expansion, while others need a slower, more measured approach.

VTBs are also an excellent solution for people who cannot qualify for a mortgage—whether due to self-employment, inconsistent income, or lack of down payment funds.

That's why negotiation is key. You need to search for VTB opportunities, and it all starts with how you approach the conversation with the seller and their agent. You won't always find a seller willing to do it, but when you do, it can be a powerful tool to acquire real estate without traditional financing.

Real estate is not about rushing to make a deal. It's about making the right deal. If you want real success in this business, align yourself with professionals who are active in the industry, who adapt to market changes, and who have a proven ability to execute.

FINAL THOUGHT
Knowledge Without Experience Is Dangerous

If you're serious about real estate investing, be selective about where you get your education. Courses and seminars can introduce concepts, but they cannot replace real-world experience. Your success depends on:

- The accuracy of your information
- The quality of your network
- Your ability to adapt to market conditions

Trust experience over hype. Work with people who do this every single day, not just those who talk about it. That's how you close the deal.

5

MASTERING THE ART
OF CLOSING DEALS

How do you close the deal? There is a lot more to it than people may think. Many aspiring investors think closing a deal is as simple as making an offer and signing paperwork. In reality, the process is filled with potential pitfalls that can make or break your investment.

THE ILLUSION OF INVESTMENT TRAINING SEMINARS

In recent years, real estate investment training seminars have become a booming industry, attracting thousands of hopeful investors with promises of financial independence. People are spending anywhere from $10,000 to $100,000 a year to be part of these exclusive training programs, expecting to walk away with a foolproof strategy for real estate success.

Here's the hard truth: many of these programs are run by individuals who lack real-world experience. Their knowledge is often theoretical, outdated, or based on a business model designed more for making money off students than actually helping them succeed.

I've seen investment groups led by individuals with no significant real estate portfolios themselves, yet they are teaching others how to build one. Their credentials? Maybe they flipped a few houses years ago, or they've memorized a scripted seminar that hasn't changed in years.

I've personally been invited as a guest speaker at these events, specifically on mortgage financing. I've met investors who have been misled by the advice they received.

MASS BIDDING: A COSTLY MISTAKE

One of the most reckless strategies I've seen promoted in these seminars is the idea of putting in as many offers as possible and seeing what sticks.

I've seen investment tour groups where people hop on a bus, visit various cities, and flood the market with offers, sometimes twenty or more at a time. These offers are often made without thorough research, without consulting experienced Realtors or mortgage brokers, and sometimes even without seeing the properties firsthand.

The instructors don't care if the offers get accepted or not. They encourage this mass bidding approach because it makes their students feel like they are taking action. What they don't realize is that this behavior:

- Wastes the time of real estate professionals (agents, brokers, sellers, and lenders)
- Damages the investor's reputation—making it harder to be taken seriously in future negotiations
- Leads to poor decision-making—as rushed offers often ignore key financial and legal risks

Many people in these programs blindly trust the process because they've already spent thousands of dollars on the training, so they feel pressured to follow through, even when their instincts tell them otherwise.

WHERE THESE PROGRAMS CAN ADD VALUE: AND WHERE THEY FAIL

I'm not saying that investment training programs are entirely useless. If used correctly, they can provide valuable networking opportunities and a broader perspective on the industry. Meeting other investors, learning about different markets, and hearing new ideas can all be beneficial. Key areas where these programs often provide misleading or incomplete advice include:

Working with real estate agents. Many investors don't understand the importance of building strong relationships with agents and instead focus on aggressive tactics that harm their reputation.

Structuring offers properly. Overloading an offer with conditions or going in firm without proper due diligence can both be costly mistakes. Navigating mortgage financing. Financing is not a one-size-fits-all process.

Shopping for the right mortgage product. The lending landscape changes weekly, making it essential to get guidance from active industry professionals.

Success in real estate doesn't come from paying for seminars or memorizing scripts, it comes from working with the right people and continuously educating yourself from real-world experience.

If you want to close deals efficiently and profitably, your inner circle should include:

- Experienced real estate agents who understand your market and your investment strategy.
- Reliable mortgage brokers who can secure financing tailored to your needs.
- Trusted legal professionals who ensure your contracts protect you.
- Seasoned investors and mentors who have a track record of real success.

People purchase memberships and attend investment training seminars taught by individuals who are not necessarily knowledgeable about what is really happening in the industry. I'm not saying that all of them lack expertise, but their knowledge is not always based on real industry experience.

For example, the head speaker of an investment training company may have 5,000 investor members eagerly awaiting great success through get-rich-quick schemes. The unfortunate part is that the majority of the trainers or coaches may not have enough experience or a portfolio that justifies them providing advice to new investors.

Having participated in these real estate investment companies as a speaker on mortgage financing for decades; I know how important it is to ensure that the information being relayed is accurate and relevant. While these seminars may offer useful networking opportunities, they often fall short in teaching the real mechanics of securing and closing a deal.

COMMON PITFALLS IN CLOSING DEALS

- Waiving financing conditions too early
- Failing to align with your broker before submitting an offer
- Ignoring red flags in listing terms that could delay funding

- Over-relying on one source of financing
- Making multiple offers without a clear strategy

You cannot rely on someone's rehearsed speech that they have been delivering for years. The mortgage and finance business changes weekly. Whether it's residential, commercial, or private financing, the guidance needs to come directly from industry professionals. People who live and breathe the business, know it intimately, and actively practice it themselves.

More often, the process unfolds like this: people write an offer, but the person writing the offer does not understand real estate investing. When the deal reaches the broker, it's a mess. They are forced to work with it because that's the reality of the situation. Now, you have two days to secure funding, yet you haven't built any relationships. You're running around, and you're at risk. In Canada, if you don't close, you could lose your deposit.

You must be fully organized. Never waive your conditions unless you receive a sign-off from your mortgage broker or bank. Even at the last minute, a financial institution can cancel your deal if something changes dramatically between your approval date and closing.

You can still attend these events to network and build your team. However, the most important thing is ensuring your financing is in order. Know exactly what you qualify for and your buying power. What should you be chasing? Your dream may be big, but it's wise to start on a smaller scale. Everyone wants to recoup their investment, and you must ensure you're not abusing industry professionals because word travels fast. Be respectful to real estate agents and others you work with. If you continually fail to close deals after submitting offers, professionals will stop taking you seriously.

FINAL THOUGHTS
The Key to Closing Deals

I once had a client who learned this lesson the hard way. He had attended a weekend seminar, followed every step to the letter, and put in multiple offers without truly understanding the financial side. When it came time to secure funding, he found himself scrambling, unable to close, and ultimately lost his deposit. After that experience, he approached the business differently. He built real relationships with professionals, did his due diligence, and ensured his financing was secure before making offers. The next time, he closed successfully.

The key to success in real estate investing isn't luck, it's preparation. The better you understand financing, deal structuring, and negotiation, the more confidently you can close deals that set you up for long-term wealth.

6

LOCATION, LOCATION, LOCATION

THE IMPORTANCE OF LOCATION: WHY WHERE YOU INVEST MATTERS

One of the most critical decisions you will ever make in real estate is where to invest. Location is not just about what looks good on paper. It is about what makes sense for you, your strategy, and your ability to scale.

When you first begin purchasing real estate, the smartest thing you can do is invest in your own backyard. That does not necessarily mean the exact city or neighborhood where you live today. It could be the place where you grew up, where you have family, or somewhere you have deep connections and someone you can trust.

If you do not have that built-in familiarity, then your next step is research. You need to do more than just Google the area. You need to understand the location—its growth potential, its desirability, its strengths and weaknesses, and most importantly, how you can build a presence there.

My philosophy in real estate has always been to buy in an area and grow in that area. There is an undeniable power in numbers. The more properties you own in one location, the more influence you have.

When you are working within an area you know, you know the truth about the neighborhood. You know the good areas and the bad areas. You know which schools are nearby, which streets are walkable, where the best amenities are, and where future development is happening.

Google can show you a map, but Google cannot tell you about desirability. It cannot give you the real picture of a neighborhood. A community may look perfect on paper, but until you physically walk the streets, talk to people, and observe the area at different times of the day, you will never know the full story.

Before you even look at deals, you need to ask yourself a fundamental question: How will I manage this property?

PROXIMITY MATTERS MORE THAN YOU THINK

The first thing to look at when choosing your investment location is your own ability to manage it. Even if you eventually hire a property manager, you still need to be able to get there when needed. If a problem arises, if something goes wrong, if there is an emergency, you need to be in control.

If you cannot manage it personally, then ask yourself, do you have someone you trust nearby who can help? Do you have friends, family, or reliable business partners in the area?

Managing real estate effectively means building a system that works, and the best way to do that is through geographical concentration.

You are not just buying one property. Eventually, you are going to buy more. The key is to choose a location where you can build a portfolio without making your life and management responsibilities a logistical nightmare.

WHY YOUR LOCATION WILL MAKE OR BREAK YOUR SUCCESS

I have seen investors make brilliant financial decisions when it comes to numbers yet fail completely because they chose a location they did not understand or could not manage efficiently.

Real estate is about more than just the property itself. The location determines everything, your tenant base, your potential appreciation, your ability to scale, and most importantly, how well you can manage the property and control your investment.

If you want to be successful in real estate, start by choosing a location you can control, scale, and dominate. Your future in this business depends on it.

THE IMPORTANCE OF LOCATION: BUILDING A FOUNDATION FOR GROWTH

When you step into real estate, you are not just buying a property. You are building an investment strategy that will determine your ability to grow, scale, and succeed in the long term. If you plan on expanding your portfolio beyond just one property, you need to think strategically about location.

It is easy to get caught up in the excitement of a deal, but if you buy randomly, one house in one city, another an hour away, and another two hours in the opposite direction. You will quickly realize that managing them is a logistical nightmare.

If you are wise in your acquisitions, you may start to see the bigger picture. Maybe you begin by buying one house in a great neighborhood, an area that is up-and-coming, being regentrified, full of potential. Then, you buy another down the street. Over time, you accumulate four or five houses on the same block. Ten years down the line, what was once a collection of single-family homes can now be a prime opportunity for redevelopment. You could tear them down and build a multi-family complex, potentially rezone the area, or sell them as a complete assembly for a major profit.

I have always been someone who looks at a property and asks myself, What's the vision here?

- Is this just going to be a single-family home?
- Am I buying this to convert into a short-term rental?
- Will I live on the main floor and rent out the basement?
- Should I be looking to acquire more properties on the street?
- Is there an opportunity to transition into multi-family development?

A property is never just a single transaction. It is a stepping stone to something bigger. To see those opportunities, you need to understand your location, research zoning laws, and investigate the future development plans of the city.

DOING YOUR HOMEWORK: HOW TO RESEARCH A NEIGHBORHOOD

If you are serious about building in an area, you need to know it inside and out. That means going beyond just checking MLS listings. Physically go into the town or city and talk to people. Walk into city hall and speak to the local councilors, meet the mayor, introduce yourself to the community leaders. Ask the politicians, "What's the plan for this neighborhood? What are the long-term development goals?" If you even get an inkling that something big might be coming.—New transit, rezoning opportunities, major infrastructure projects; that might be your cue to buy.

I have spent hours researching neighborhoods before making an investment. I go onto city websites, dig into zoning laws, check for population growth statistics, and look at development plans. Google Earth has been one of my greatest tools. I "walk" down the streets of a city before I even visit it in person.

I recently bought a second property in Fort Myers, Florida, and before I made the decision, I spent weeks studying the area. I walked through every street virtually, mapped out everything I needed to know, and fully understood the neighborhood's trajectory before making my move.

CAPITALIZING ON CHANGE: HOW SHIFTING REAL ESTATE RULES CREATE OPPORTUNITY

The rules around real estate are always changing, and for investors who pay attention, these changes can create massive opportunities.

Take Canada, due to the ongoing housing crisis, the government has now made it legal to convert garages into secondary dwelling units. This means homeowners can now add rental suites without having to go through the same red tape and zoning restrictions that once made it nearly impossible.

Back in the early 2000s, if you put a basement apartment in your home and it wasn't legally permitted, you could be forced to remove it entirely. Today, with the overwhelming demand for housing, the government is actively encouraging these conversions, approving them without hesitation.

Savvy investors should pay close attention to these shifts. Every city, province, and state has its own rules, and these rules are constantly evolving. If you can anticipate what's coming, you can position yourself ahead of the market and capitalize on new opportunities before they become mainstream.

SHORT-TERM VS. LONG-TERM RENTALS: WHICH ONE IS RIGHT FOR YOU?

The type of rental strategy you choose is just as important as the location itself.

Long-term rentals are often the simplest to manage. You might encounter difficult tenants, it's part of the business. Once a lease is signed, your income is stable, predictable, and requires less daily oversight.

Short-term rentals, on the other hand, can generate significantly higher revenue. In my experience, my vacation rentals and short-term rentals generate twenty to thirty percent more net income compared to traditional long-term leases.

There's a catch. Short-term rentals require constant attention, higher maintenance costs, and ongoing management expenses. You have to deal with frequent guest turnovers, cleaning fees, marketing efforts, and strict local regulations that can change overnight.

Many cities are now restricting short-term rentals as they are seen as competition to hotels. Some municipalities have banned Airbnbs entirely, while others allow them only if they are owner-occupied properties. If you're considering investing in a short-term rental, thoroughly research the local laws before making a purchase.

Long-term rentals come with a different set of risks, particularly when it comes to landlord and tenant regulations. Ontario has some of the most restrictive landlord-tenant laws in North America. Once you have a long-term tenant, your ability to remove them is extremely limited, even in cases of non-payment.

One of the biggest mistakes new investors make is closing on a property without securing vacant possession. If a tenant is already living in the property, depending on the laws in your region, you may not have any legal right to ask them to leave after closing. If you need the property vacant, make sure it's vacant before you buy.

THE BOTTOM LINE

The most successful investors are the ones who stay ahead of evolving regulations, market trends, and investment strategies. Whether it's zoning changes, rental laws, new financing rules, or government incentives, those who can pivot and capitalize on these shifts will always come out ahead.

LESSONS FROM MY OWN MISTAKES

When I started investing, I did not always follow my own rules.

At first, I bought properties close to home, where I knew the neighborhoods and had relationships in place. As my confidence grew, I got too excited, too fast. I ventured into Windsor, Ontario, even though I lived in Burlington. I bought properties without knowing the neighborhoods, without knowing the right people, and without even seeing the properties firsthand. I ended up losing money because I hadn't taken the time to truly research what or where I was buying. I was too eager to jump in, and I did learn, but the hard way.

For every mistake, there were wins that far outweighed the losses. What I gained through those experiences was invaluable knowledge that shaped how I invest today.

UNDERSTANDING ZONING BEFORE YOU BUY

One of the first three properties I bought, I decided to move my office into it. My real estate agent at the time told me that the zoning allowed for both an office and a rental unit. I set up my business on the main floor, rented out the upper unit, and everything was going great.

Until the city came knocking. They informed me that I was not allowed to operate my business there and that the second rental unit was not legal. I had spent time and money renovating, setting up my business, and getting everything in place. Only to find out after the fact that I wasn't legally permitted to do what I had planned.

I ended up selling the property. Thankfully, I made a profit, but it was still a hard lesson in trusting information without verifying it myself.

From that moment on, I double-check zoning regulations, approvals, and legalities before making a move. No matter who tells me something is "approved" or "allowed," I confirm it myself. A simple oversight can cost a fortune in wasted time and money.

BUILDING RELATIONSHIPS IN YOUR INVESTMENT AREA

One of the smartest things you can do when investing in a new market is build relationships with the local community.

I once bought a fifteen unit apartment building in a small town in Ontario, with plans to convert it into condos. Small-town politics can be tough. They didn't know me, and they didn't trust me. I knew that if I wanted to get approvals, permits, and community support, I needed to earn their trust.

So, once a week, for months, I drove down there with homemade apple strudel, cheesecakes, or doughnuts for the city officials. Over time, I built relationships, showed that I was invested in the community, and in the end, I got the approvals I needed.

You have to immerse yourself in the community. Get involved, support local causes, and become a name people recognize and trust. Real estate isn't just about buying properties. It's about investing in the neighborhood itself.

7

GRADUATING TO COMMERCIAL PROPERTIES

After years of investing in residential real estate, buying triplexes, duplexes, single-family homes, and experimenting with short-term and long-term rentals, you start asking yourself a fundamental question: Is it better to have more units under one roof than to own 100 roofs and 100 furnaces?

There comes a point when managing multiple small properties becomes inefficient. The more you grow, the more you start to recognize the value of scale, fewer individual properties, but with a much larger number of units under one roof. The industry consensus is that once you surpass thirty units, the benefits of economies of scale truly kick in.

THE ROADBLOCK IN RESIDENTIAL FINANCING

For investors in Canada, there is an added challenge when continuing to acquire residential properties: financing limitations.

Banks cap how many properties they are willing to lend on. Typically, once you have five mortgages in your name, it becomes increasingly difficult to obtain financing. Even if you have the cash flow, even if you have the net worth, the institutions start closing their doors on further lending.

This is where investors start looking toward commercial real estate, not necessarily because they planned to, they have no other choice if they want to keep growing.

If you are a husband-and-wife team or working with a business partner, it is critical to structure your mortgages separately. Many investors make the mistake of applying for financing together on every property. The problem with this is that when you go to buy another one, both of your names are tied to all previous mortgages, making it difficult to qualify for more.

A better approach is to split the loans between partners. One of you takes on five properties, the other takes on another five. This way, instead of being capped at five mortgages total, you now have access to ten.

Even this strategy has limits. At a certain point, institutional lending stops being an option, and many investors are forced to use private money as a bridge to continue growing. While private money is a great tool, it is significantly more expensive than traditional financing. It is not a long-term solution, it should only be used when the deal is strong enough that the cost of financing is worth the opportunity.

This is why having strong relationships with lenders and brokers is key. You always need to have a funding source in your back pocket for when the right deal comes along.

If residential real estate is still your direction, there is another route you can take, transitioning your portfolio into a corporate structure and financing through commercial lenders. This comes with higher interest rates and a more intensive underwriting process, but it can unlock more funding opportunities.

THE COMMERCIAL LENDING SHIFT

Unlike residential real estate, commercial financing is not about your personal income. In commercial lending, you qualify based on the income of the building itself. It is strictly numbers-driven.

The bank will analyze the debt service ratios, meaning they look at how much money the property generates versus how much the mortgage payments will be. The stronger the cash flow, the easier it is to finance.

This is one of the reasons why so many investors eventually move into commercial real estate.

If I go to a bank and try to get $10 million in residential mortgages, they will likely reject me after a certain number of deals. If I bring them a $10 million commercial property with strong financials, I can easily secure financing. The building is paying for itself.

In Canada, anything over six units is considered commercial real estate, even if it is an apartment building. Commercial lending covers much more than just multifamily properties—it includes industrial, office buildings, retail plazas, hotels, and other asset classes.

The financing process is entirely different from residential. Instead of looking at the borrower's income and liabilities, lenders focus on three primary things:

First, your credit must be strong. Commercial financing often involves larger loan amounts, and banks are taking greater risks. If your credit history is weak, you will struggle to get an institutional mortgage.

Second, your experience matters. If you are applying for a multimillion-dollar loan, banks want to see a track record of successfully managing properties. They may require you to submit a bio or CV, detailing your real estate experience, past investments, and management history. In some cases, banks will even reject a deal if they do not trust the property manager you are working with.

Third, the property's income is the ultimate deciding factor. In commercial real estate, the value of a building is determined by the income it generates. Location, condition, and other factors still matter, but the main driver of financing approval is whether the property can service the debt.

WHY INVESTORS MOVE TO COMMERCIAL

Once you understand how commercial real estate is financed, you begin to see why so many investors eventually make the transition. Residential real estate has strict limitations. It is tied to personal income, credit restrictions, and financing caps that eventually slow down your ability to grow. In contrast, commercial real estate offers bigger opportunities, larger funding options, and a pathway to significantly scale your portfolio.

When you buy a single-family home, its value is largely determined by comparable sales, what other homes in the area have sold for. You have very little control over how much it is worth.

When you buy a commercial property, its value is tied directly to the income it produces. If you increase rents, cut expenses, or improve management efficiency, you can dramatically increase the property's value.

This is why large-scale investors focus on commercial assets. Instead of being at the mercy of the residential market, they can force appreciation by increasing net operating income.

THE SHIFT FROM RESIDENTIAL TO COMMERCIAL

For many investors, transitioning to commercial real estate is a natural progression.

At first, you start with single-family homes. You experiment with duplexes, triplexes, and small multi-units. You test short-term rentals, long-term rentals, and value-add renovations.

If you are serious about expanding your portfolio, at some point, you will likely make the move to commercial investing. The process is different, the financing is different, and the management style is different, but the rewards can be significantly greater.

Understanding the financial structure, debt servicing, and income potential of commercial real estate is key to making that transition successfully.

FINAL THOUGHTS
The Power of Scaling

The more properties you own, the more you realize the importance of structure, financing, and efficiency. Residential investing is where you learn, but commercial real estate is where you scale.

The key to long-term success in real estate is always thinking ahead. If you are still in the early stages of investing, begin by focusing on growth within a specific market, mastering management, and understanding financing.

If you have mastered residential investing, the next step is understanding commercial financing, developing relationships with lenders, and preparing for the shift into bigger assets.

8

THE POWER OF CASH FLOW

I have created a go-to cash flow analysis sheet that I have used for over twenty-five years, and what makes me laugh is that I see it everywhere now. It is like my secret formula somehow got out, and now, it has become the industry standard. I have seen my exact framework being used by brokers, investors, banks, and real estate agents. It is in presentations, spreadsheets, and investment packages. Cash flow can be found at www.feelthedeal.com.

A cash flow statement is the single most important tool in determining whether a deal will work, not just for you, but for the bank. If you cannot prove that a deal will financially sustain itself, you are either not getting financing or you are walking into a money pit.

THE ANATOMY OF A CASH FLOW STATEMENT

Every real estate deal starts with one fundamental thing: income.

You begin by calculating the total rental income from each and every unit in the building. Then, you factor in vacancy rates.

Some investors make the mistake of saying, "My building is fully occupied, so I have zero vacancy." That is not how lenders or experienced investors think.

Even the best buildings have turnover, maintenance downtime, and occasional vacancies. A lender will expect you to include at least a one to two percent vacancy rate, and this number should reflect real market data. You can Google vacancy rates in your area, check reports from the city, or speak to local property managers for insights.

Once you deduct vacancies from your rental income, you are left with your gross effective income; the real amount you are working with.

UNDERSTANDING EXPENSES: THE HIDDEN COSTS YOU MUST ACCOUNT FOR

This is where things start to get dangerous if you do not know what you are doing.

When real estate agents market a property, they often provide only the most basic expenses. They will tell you about the property taxes, insurance, and utilities, but they will never tell you the real operating costs that impact cash flow.

Sellers do this, too. They will hand you a spreadsheet that looks great on paper, but when you dig deeper, you realize that half the actual expenses are missing. If you do not investigate the full cost of running a building, you could find yourself bleeding money from the moment you close the deal.

Here are the real costs you must account for:

PROPERTY TAXES

This is one of the biggest hidden dangers in real estate. When someone has owned a property for thirty years, their property taxes are often artificially low. They have been grandfathered in, and their taxes have barely moved. The moment you buy the property, the city reassesses the value, and suddenly, your tax bill skyrockets. Always check the tax rate for the area and calculate what your taxes will be after you buy, not just what they are today.

INSURANCE

Do not trust the insurance quote provided by the seller. It is often outdated, underreported, or simply incorrect. Lenders will require your own insurance quote, and if you do not have an accurate number, your financing could be jeopardized at the last minute. I have seen deals where the seller claimed insurance was $1,500 per year, and then, right before closing, the new quote came in at $9,000 per year. That kind of jump can kill your financing and put you in a bad position instantly.

MAINTENANCE COSTS

Lenders typically assume a minimum of $700 per unit per year in maintenance. That means if you buy a twenty unit building, the bank expects that you will be spending at least $14,000 annually in upkeep. This money goes toward unit turnovers, painting, repairs, and general upkeep. If you are not budgeting for this, you are not being realistic.

PROPERTY MANAGEMENT FEES

Even if you plan to self-manage, lenders do not care. The bank will automatically factor in property management costs because if you default on the loan, they will need to hire someone to take over. Most lenders will assume five percent of gross effective income will go toward management fees, and if your building is large enough, you may be able to negotiate that down to three percent.

ADDITIONAL INCOME SOURCES THAT CAN BOOST YOUR NUMBERS

Rental income is not the only way to generate cash flow from a property. Many investors fail to maximize their income potential because they overlook small revenue streams that add up significantly over time.

- Does your property have a parking lot? Charge for parking.
- Do tenants need storage space? Offer storage lockers.
- Is there signage space available? Lease it to local businesses.
- Do you own a laundry facility? Make sure the machines are coin-operated or tied to a revenue sharing agreement.
- Every dollar of additional income increases your net operating income, which in turn raises the value of your property.

THE CAP RATE: HOW COMMERCIAL PROPERTIES ARE VALUED

One of the biggest differences between residential and commercial real estate is how properties are valued.

In commercial real estate, the value of the property is determined by its income, not comparable sales. This is where the cap rate comes into play.

A cap rate is the return an investor expects from a property, based on its net operating income (NOI). Cap rates vary based on location, interest rates, and property type. If you are in a high-demand area like Burlington, cap rates might be four to five percent. If you are in a riskier market, cap rates may be higher, meaning the property is cheaper relative to its income.

HOW FINANCING WORKS IN COMMERCIAL REAL ESTATE

Now that you have your cash flow statement, you can determine how much financing you qualify for.

Banks will lend based on the debt coverage ratio (DCR). This is the ratio of a property's net income to its mortgage payments.

Most banks require a DCR of 1.1 to 1.3, meaning your property must generate ten to thirty percent more income than the annual mortgage payments.

If your NOI is $100,000, and you are looking for a $2 million mortgage, the bank will check to see if your DCR meets their requirements. If not, they will reduce the loan amount, forcing you to come up with a larger down payment.

This is why running your numbers properly is critical. If you do not assess your financing before making an offer, you might find out too late that you cannot close the deal.

THE POWER OF CASH FLOW ANALYSIS

For twenty-five years, my cash flow statement has been my most valuable tool in real estate. It tells me if a deal works or not, if I can get financing, and if the numbers make sense.

If you take the time to run the numbers, break down every expense, and understand how banks assess a deal, you will never be surprised.

MAXIMIZING CASH FLOW: UNDERSTANDING EVERY INCOME SOURCE AND EXPENSE

One of the greatest mistakes an investor can make is underestimating income potential and overlooking expenses. A building is not just about rent collected, there are often hidden revenue streams that, when optimized, can significantly increase the value of your property.

At the same time, failing to properly assess expenses can turn what seems like a great deal on paper into a financial nightmare. Sellers and real estate agents will often present only the most basic expenses, leaving out critical costs that could eat away at your bottom line.

UNLOCKING ADDITIONAL INCOME STREAMS

Most investors look at a building's rental income and stop there. A smart investor looks for opportunities to increase cash flow in ways that other people overlook.

Signage income is a great example. If you own a commercial or mixed-use building, you may be able to rent out exterior wall space or rooftop advertising to local businesses. Even in residential buildings, I have seen investors lease signage space to companies promoting local services.

Laundry income is another source of additional revenue. In older apartment buildings, many investors install coin-operated laundry machines or set up partnerships with laundry service companies that manage everything in exchange for a revenue split. This is a passive, easy way to generate extra income.

Parking lot income is another big one. If your property has extra parking spaces, you can rent them out separately. This applies especially if you are located near a downtown core, a high-demand area, or a transit hub. Some investors even lease out parking spaces to non-tenants if local businesses or commuters are looking for parking options.

Storage locker income is often overlooked, yet tenants are more than willing to pay extra for secure storage space. If your building has a basement or unused space, converting it into tenant storage lockers can provide additional revenue with little to no extra maintenance.

UTILITY COSTS: WHO PAYS?

One of the biggest expenses that landlords fail to assess properly is utilities. Are the tenants paying for their own utilities, or are all utilities included in the rent?

If the utilities are not separately metered, you are likely paying for everything, which can be extremely costly. Separately metering utilities is one of the best investments you can make because it shifts the cost to the tenant and incentivizes them to be more energy-efficient.

If it is not practical to individually meter each unit, consider installing mini-split heating and cooling systems so that tenants are responsible for their own energy costs. Even if it requires an upfront investment, this can drastically reduce your operating expenses in the long run.

Do not forget water costs. Many investors overlook water when calculating expenses, but it can be a significant monthly bill.

GARBAGE COLLECTION: AN EASILY OVERLOOKED EXPENSE

Garbage collection is another hidden cost that sellers often fail to mention. Do you have a private garbage bin, or is the trash picked up at the curb?

If the property has dumpsters, those have monthly costs. If trash is collected at the curb, you need to find out who is responsible for taking it out every week. If there is no superintendent, you may need to hire someone or do it yourself, which means time and expense.

SUPERINTENDENTS AND BUILDING MAINTENANCE STAFF

If your building is large enough, you might need an on-site superintendent or maintenance manager. This person handles tenant concerns, minor repairs, and keeps the building in good condition.

The cost of a superintendent is often left out of a seller's expense reports. They may not have had one, or they may have been paying under-market wages, which you will not be able to sustain long-term.

SNOW REMOVAL, LANDSCAPING, AND BUILDING CLEANING

Many investors fail to properly budget for snow removal, landscaping, and cleaning services.

If your building has sidewalks, parking lots, or green spaces, these will require ongoing maintenance. These services are not cheap. Snow removal, in particular, can be extremely costly in harsh winters. The last thing you want is to be caught off guard by high seasonal expenses that you failed to budget for.

Get your own market quotes for these services instead of relying on numbers provided by the seller.

CLEANING AND SECURITY

If your property has common areas, hallways, or shared spaces, you will need a professional cleaning service to keep everything well-maintained.

Having a clean building attracts better tenants, reduces turnover, and maintains property value. A neglected building leads to vacancies, tenant complaints, and higher maintenance costs in the long run.

In some cases, buildings may require security services, especially if they are located in high-traffic or downtown areas. Some larger properties opt for security patrols, controlled access systems, or on-site security personnel. These costs must be factored into your cash flow analysis.

GETTING THE SELLER'S FINANCIALS: THE KEY TO VERIFYING THE DEAL

One of the smartest things you can do before buying a building is to request two to three years of past financial statements and at least twelve months of utility bills. The seller is not required to provide this information, but refusal is a red flag.

Having these records allows you to go through real historical numbers and verify whether the income and expenses match what has been presented to you.

Too often, sellers will show pro forma numbers, meaning projections or estimates, rather than the actual financials. These estimates are often wildly inaccurate and designed to make the deal look more attractive than it really is.

HOW CASH FLOW DETERMINES A PROPERTY'S VALUE

Once you have all income and expenses calculated, you arrive at the net operating income (NOI)—the true profitability of the building.

Typically, expenses should fall between thirty to forty percent of your gross income. If expenses are significantly higher, you need to dig deeper into the reasons why.

This is where the cap rate comes into play. The cap rate (capitalization rate) determines the market value of a property based on its income.

If your NOI is $100,000 per year, and the market cap rate is five percent, the formula to calculate the property value is:

$100,000 \div 0.05 = \$2,000,000$

The cap rate is influenced by interest rates, location, condition, and property type. A lower cap rate means a higher price, while a higher cap rate means the property is more affordable relative to its income.

FINAL THOUGHTS
Why a Strong Cash Flow Analysis is Everything

If there is one thing that separates successful investors from those who fail, it is the ability to accurately analyze cash flow.

For over twenty-five years, my cash flow analysis sheet has been the foundation of my investment decisions. It tells me whether a deal works, whether I can get financing, and whether the numbers truly make sense.

If you trust a seller's financials without verifying them, if you fail to include hidden expenses, or if you do not factor in realistic vacancy rates and future cost increases, you are gambling with your investment.

If you take the time to run the numbers correctly, verify every income and expense, and understand how lenders evaluate cash flow, you will always know whether a deal is worth pursuing.

That is the difference between investors who thrive and those who lose everything.

9

THE POWER OF THE CAP RATE AND STRUCTURING FINANCING FOR SUCCESS

Now that you have gathered all of your income and expenses, accounted for vacancy rates, and calculated your net operating income (NOI), you are ready for the next critical step, determining the true value of the property.

UNDERSTANDING THE CAP RATE: THE FORMULA THAT DETERMINES VALUE

In commercial real estate, a property's value is not determined by comparable sales like in residential real estate. Instead, it is based on a simple formula using the capitalization rate.

Let's say your net operating income is $100,000 per year, and you are in a high-demand city like Burlington.

If cap rates in that area are around four to five percent, the value of your property would be calculated as follows:

$100,000 ÷ 0.05 = $2,000,000

This means that if a property generates $100,000 in annual NOI, and the market cap rate is five percent, the property is worth $2 million.

WHAT DETERMINES A CAP RATE?

A cap rate is not a fixed number, it fluctuates based on several factors:

- Interest rates—When interest rates rise, cap rates tend to rise, which lowers property values. When interest rates fall, cap rates tend to drop, increasing property values.
- Location—Desirable, high-demand areas have lower cap rates, making properties more expensive.
- Building condition—A well-maintained, modern building typically trades at a lower cap rate than a run-down or outdated property.
- Asset type—A multifamily apartment building will often have a different cap rate than an office, retail, or industrial property.
- Market demand—If investors are flooding into a particular asset class or region, cap rates will compress, meaning properties become more expensive.

A simple way to determine cap rates in a market is to ask local commercial real estate agents. If you are buying a multifamily building, ask, "What is the current cap rate for multifamily properties in this city?" If you are looking at an office building, do the same.

WHAT A CAP RATE TELLS YOU ABOUT A DEAL

If a seller is asking for a three percent cap rate on a building that should be trading at a five percent cap, that means the asking price is too high.

The lower the cap rate, the more expensive the property. The higher the cap rate, the cheaper it is in relation to its income. Finding a property at a higher cap rate is a huge win, because it means you are getting more income per dollar spent.

THE VALUE OF STABILIZING A PROPERTY

One of the best opportunities in commercial real estate is finding a mismanaged property with rents far below market value.

Imagine you find a fifteen unit building where tenants have been living there for twenty years, paying way below market rent. That might sound like a good thing at first, but if rent is significantly under market value, it could take years to turn over tenants and bring the building to its full earning potential.

On the other hand, if a fifteen unit building is half vacant, that could be an opportunity. You could immediately rent out the empty units at market rates, increasing the property's net operating income, which in turn increases its overall value.

If you have a tenant paying $800 per month, but the market rent for that unit is $1,600, that means you have $800 per month in upside per unit.

Now, let's calculate how that affects the property's value:

- $800 × twelve months = $9,600 in additional annual income
- $9,600 ÷ five percent cap rate = $192,000 in added property value

That means that by raising the rent to market value, you have increased the building's worth by $192,000 per unit. If you repeat that across multiple units, you can create millions of dollars in additional property value just by managing the building correctly.

This is the true power of commercial real estate. Every dollar added to the bottom line significantly increases the overall value of the property.

FINANCING A COMMERCIAL PROPERTY: HOW IT WORKS

Once you have calculated your NOI and cap rate, you now need to determine how much financing you can get.

In commercial real estate, banks do not lend based on your personal income, they lend based on the property's ability to pay for itself.

One of the biggest factors is interest rates. Let's say today's conventional mortgage rates are at six percent, and banks are offering twenty-five year amortization terms.

Here's how the numbers play out:

If a property has an NOI of $100,000 per year, and it is valued at $2 million at a five percent cap rate, you might want to finance seventy-five percent of that purchase price, which would be a $1.5 million mortgage.

DEBT COVERAGE RATIO: HOW THE BANK DETERMINES LOAN AMOUNTS

Banks use a debt coverage ratio (DCR) to ensure that a property's income is sufficient to cover the mortgage payments. The formula is simple:

Debt Coverage Ratio = Net Operating Income ÷ Annual Mortgage Payments

Let's say:

- Your NOI is $100,000
- Your annual mortgage payments are $90,000
  $100,000 ÷ $90,000 = 1.1 DCR

Most banks require a DCR between 1.1 and 1.3.

If your DCR is too low, the bank will not give you the full loan amount you are requesting, meaning you will need more money for the down payment.

This is why running your numbers in advance is so critical. You need to know before making an offer how much financing you are actually going to get.

NEGOTIATING CREATIVE FINANCING: THE VENDOR TAKE-BACK (VTB) STRATEGY

If the bank is not willing to give you seventy-five percent financing, and they only offer sixty-five percent, you might find yourself short on cash for the down payment.

This is where a vendor take-back mortgage (VTB) can be a game-changer. You go to the seller and say, "I love this property, but the bank will only finance sixty-five percent. Would you be willing to hold a second mortgage for the remaining ten percent?"

Depending on market conditions, you might even negotiate a competitive interest rate, say three or five percent on that second mortgage.

If the bank does not allow second mortgages, you can negotiate a creative structure. Instead of holding the mortgage on the property you are buying, the seller can hold the loan against another property you own. That way, it does not affect the debt coverage ratio, and you still secure the financing you need.

FINAL THOUGHTS
The Power of Cash Flow and Financing Strategy

If you know how to calculate NOI, cap rates, DCR, and financing options, you have everything you need to determine whether a deal is worth pursuing.

If you understand how to structure deals, negotiate financing, and maximize cash flow, you will always be one step ahead. That is how you win in commercial real estate.

Unlike in residential real estate, where the number of mortgages you can get is capped by your personal income, in commercial real estate, you could finance a $10 million property more easily than a $5 million portfolio of residential homes.

10

THE REALITY OF COMMERCIAL REAL ESTATE
FINANCING, DUE DILIGENCE, AND LESSONS FROM THE TRENCHES

Moving from residential real estate into commercial investing is a completely different game. The numbers are larger, the financing is more complex, and the due diligence process is significantly more intensive.

If you have been buying single-family homes or small multifamily properties, you may have already hit the residential financing cap. Many banks limit borrowers to five mortgages before they start making it increasingly difficult to borrow. At that point, investors often transition into commercial real estate.

THE SHIFT TO COMMERCIAL LENDING
Once you have assessed a commercial deal and want to proceed, you must understand that there are significant upfront costs. Unlike in residential deals where you might

only need an appraisal, commercial financing involves much more.

Knowing that if you are proceeding on the deal, you need to have an environmental assessment to know if there's any possible contamination and building condition reports. There are specific companies that come in and assess capital cost over the next one to ten years. You'll be hiring an appraisal company that is recommended by the mortgage broker, because you need to make sure that it is a legitimate appraisal that is regarded by the institution. It takes two to three weeks to get one done. Environmentally now, if the property is in a residential neighborhood, and there's no indicators of any kind of gas station or anything in the past, you may be able to get away with a declaration. If it happens to be in the city, and it's a busy area, chances are you need one. It's in your best interest as well. If you don't have that, and you find out that there is contamination, then it'll be very hard to finance, even with private money, and you don't want to know that last minute.

- A commercial appraisal (costing between $3,000 and $20,000)
- An environmental assessment (if applicable, another $5,000 to $15,000)
- A building condition report (typically $2,000 to $8,000)
- Legal fees, broker fees, and lender deposits

Before you even close, you could be looking at tens of thousands of dollars in due diligence costs and this is why you must be 100 percent sure about the deal before moving forward.

Banks do not pay mortgage brokers like they do in a typical easy A class deal in residential financing. Most Mortgage Brokers only get paid upon a successful closing, so they will often charge an upfront fee to ensure that they are not working for free, as once the borrower has invested in a deposit chances are they will not shop around with other banks or mortgage brokers. This type of financing will take months to put together. A commercial mortgage broker could charge anywhere from 0.5 to two percent of the loan amount, while the bank itself may charge an additional lender fee ranging from 0.2 to one percent.

For example, on a $1.5 million loan, you could be looking at:

- $15,000 to $30,000 for the broker fee
- Another $7,000 for the bank's fee
- $7,000 to $10,000 for the appraisal
- $5,000 to $10,000 for environmental reports
- $2,500 to $5,000 for legal fees to review contracts.

Before spending that kind of money, you need to be certain the deal is worth it. One of the biggest mistakes new commercial investors make is underestimating the importance of due diligence.

If a property has environmental issues (such as past contamination, leaking underground storage tanks, or prior industrial use), it can become extremely difficult to finance. Even if you find contamination after closing, you are now legally responsible for it. That means cleaning it up, remediating the site, and dealing with the city, which can cost hundreds of thousands of dollars.

Building condition reports are another essential part of the process. If a roof needs replacing, the electrical is outdated, or the structure has issues, the bank may say: "We'll finance it, but we're holding back money until you fix these problems." Typically a building condition report is part of the required documents for a commercial bank approval.

The smart move is to do an appraisal and a building condition report first. If something major is uncovered, you may decide not to move forward with the deal, which saves you from losing money on additional reports.

Even after completing your due diligence, there is always a chance that the bank will ultimately say no. If that happens, you can often sell your reports to the next buyer or even back to the seller. You need to be strategic, if you back out after paying deposits to the lender, broker, and legal teams, those costs could be considered earned, and you may not get them back. You have to decide early in the process whether you are fully committed to the deal.

When you get into properties that are commercial, and you're doing your due diligence, it's really important to make sure that you have the income verified. You're going to ask for copies of leases, for a copy of the rent roll, for financial statements. Sometimes sellers won't give you the financial statements, but I think it's a very critical piece. If they don't, then you need to make sure that you get confirmation of income and expenses. Now there's some pretty shady characters in our world.

THE BURGER DISASTER:
A PAINFUL LESSON IN DUE DILIGENCE

As I said before, I was a jump in and learn kind of investor. I believed in taking action first and figuring things out along the way. Nothing would drive that lesson home harder than the Burger disaster.

I was young, eager, and ready to take on my biggest deal yet. Two apartment buildings in Chatham, Ontario. One was fifty units, the other thirty-five units. I bought them from a man named Mr. Burger. On paper, the deal looked incredible.

I had done my walkthroughs. The buildings weren't perfect, but they had huge units, tons of character, and were right on the Thames River. The buildings were built in the 1950s, solid structures with great views. I could see the finished product in my mind.

I also received all the due diligence documents, rent rolls, income statements, and expense reports. The deal had been approved for an insured mortgage program, so I felt like I had covered my bases.

What I didn't see was the trap I was walking into. Mr. Burger was waiting for a newer, eager investor to take advantage of. This is the perfect example of why you should always trust your gut.

There were signs, small things that didn't sit right, little warnings in my mind telling me to walk away. I ignored them. The pride of owning such a large deal clouded my judgment. I let the excitement of acquiring bigger buildings get in the way of making a smart decision.

The day I took possession, I walked into what can only be described as a nightmare. The buildings were practically empty. The few tenants that were still there were crackheads. The entire place was infested with bedbugs. I had never in my life seen a property so mismanaged, so filthy, and so completely falling apart. I walked into one of the units, looked down at my feet, and watched bugs crawl onto my shoes and legs.

I started calling around, trying to figure out what the heck happened. How could these buildings go from fully occupied and performing well to completely abandoned and in ruins overnight? That's when I learned what a phantom tenant was. Mr. Burger had fabricated the rent roll. The tenants I saw during my walkthroughs? FAKE.

He had placed temporary people in the units just long enough to make the buildings look occupied. Some units were staged to appear lived in. The rent roll had been manipulated. I should have had someone go door to door, talking to the tenants before closing. That isn't always standard practice, but given the size of the deal, it should have been done. There were also tenant estoppels, which are legally required documents verifying tenants and lease terms. Those, too, were fraudulently prepared.

To make matters worse, these buildings were over two hours away from my home. This is why I always advise either buying locally or having a trusted team in place before investing in a new area.

I couldn't service the mortgages, and I had no choice but to sell. I sold the buildings at a loss, just enough to cover the reports, closing costs, and legal fees. The new buyer was able to assume my mortgages and take over the corporations I had just established.

Always trust your gut, double-check everything, and never let pride cloud your judgment.

THE DEAL THAT WOULDN'T DIE: THE NIGHTMARE OF MORTGAGE ASSUMPTION

As if the Burger deal wasn't bad enough, it came back to haunt me for years, even after I had sold the buildings and walked away.

A lawyer from Windsor bought the properties and did a share purchase of the companies, assuming the existing CMHC-insured mortgages. Since he had taken over the corporations and the debts, I assumed that meant I was no longer liable for the mortgage.

I had lost money on the deal, but at least I was done with it. I had washed my hands of the buildings, and I was ready to move on. Three months later, the bank called. "Mr. Windsor is going bankrupt. You're still responsible for the debt."

I couldn't believe what I was hearing. I had sold the properties. I had moved on; but I had never fully removed my name from the mortgage liability, I was still tied to it.

I fought it. I called my lawyer. I tried everything. The fine print was clear, I was still on the hook.

I guess this is where having a good (and expensive) lawyer comes into play. This was a hard, expensive, and painful lesson. If there's one piece of advice I want anyone reading this book to take away, it's this:

NEVER ASSUME A MORTGAGE WITHOUT FULL RELEASE

If you ever sell a property where the buyer assumes your mortgage, you must ensure that your name is completely removed from the contract. You need to be fully discharged from all obligations, with absolutely no strings attached.

Had I done that, I would have walked away clean. Instead, I ended up being dragged back into a financial mess I had nothing to do with. The worst part? I thought I had done everything right.

The buyer had passed all CMHC qualifications. He was a lawyer, a successful professional, someone who should have had no trouble making payments. Yet, three months later, he defaulted. Suddenly, I was the one stuck cleaning up the mess.

If you ever find yourself in a situation where someone wants to assume your mortgage, do not take it lightly. Make sure your name is 100 percent removed from liability. Hire a lawyer who understands mortgage assumption contracts and have them verify every single detail. If you don't, you could find yourself in the exact same nightmare I did.

Lesson Learned: Never assume a mortgage without full release.

11

THE $11 MILLION BET
BEATING THE ODDS IN REAL ESTATE

Let's talk about why I love real estate and how you can make a lot of money in it.

Real estate isn't just about the challenges, it's about opportunity, strategy, and the wins that make everything worth it. I've made millions in this business, and one of the best deals of my career happened in 2007, when I was thirty-two years old, hungry, and determined.

It's crazy how much energy we have in our younger years. Back then, I wasn't afraid of big deals. I was chasing major opportunities, and I was willing to take risks others wouldn't. That's when I found the medical plaza in Kitchener, Ontario.

THE BIGGEST DEAL OF MY LIFE (AT THE TIME)

This wasn't just any property, it was a 4.5-acre medical plaza, located in a high-traffic area with established tenants. It had been around for years, with a mix of medical offices, retail shops, and big-name fast-food chains like Taco Bell and Pizza Hut. The moment I saw it, I knew this was a deal for me.

There was one big obstacle, the owner. The building was owned by a German businessman, Mr. Jagermiester, with a reputation. Everyone in the industry warned me, "Carmen, be careful with this guy. He's tough. He plays hardball." I didn't care. I had a feeling. When I get that *Feel the Deal* moment, I trust it.

THE NEGOTIATION: A SHOWDOWN AT THE BOARDROOM TABLE

The owner was asking $11.5 million for the building, which at the time was a massive number for me. It felt like $100 million does to me today. People thought I was insane for even considering it. They kept saying, "You're nuts for paying that price."

I went to him with a proposal. I wanted a vendor take-back mortgage. I wanted him to finance the deal. I told him I would buy it for almost full price, but I needed a first mortgage covering ninety percent of the purchase price.

He studied me. Then he said, "Come to my office. We'll discuss it." I walked into his massive boardroom, a twenty foot long table separating us. He sat at one end. I sat at the other. It was intimidation at its finest.

This was a man who had seen it all in real estate. He had been in business for decades, and here I was a young, ambitious thirty-two year-old woman, sitting across from him, negotiating an eight-figure deal.

I could tell he was certain I was going to fail. To him, I was just another eager investor who would overpromise and underdeliver. He had nothing to lose. He structured this deal in a way that, if I couldn't pull off the financing, he would take the building right back, along with all the payments I had made in the meantime. This was a high-stakes game, and he thought he had stacked the odds against me.

Then he leaned forward and asked, "Tell me, why should I give you a mortgage? How do you know you're going to finance this deal?" I could feel him testing me. He wanted to see if I would flinch, if I would doubt myself for even a second.

I looked him straight in the eye and said, "Because I'm going to make this deal happen."

He leaned back, thought about it for a moment, then finally said, "Fine. I will give you the mortgage. I will sell it to you for $11.3 million. In two years, if you do not pay me out on exactly this date, my property management company will step in, issue notices to all tenants, and they will start paying me again. Everything you've invested, every payment you've made, gone. It all reverts back to me."

I had two years to replace his financing or lose everything. I shook his hand and said, "Let's do it."

CLOSING THE DEAL WITH BORROWED FUNDS AND MY OWN CASH

When the deal closed, I only had to come in with ten percent, which was incredibly rare for a deal of this size. The down payment didn't just come from my own cash. I pulled funds from my other real estate holdings, strategically leveraging borrowed money along with my own capital to make it work. This was the biggest deal of my career at the time, and I had pulled it off with minimal capital upfront.

THE TWO-YEAR RACE TO CREATE VALUE

From the moment I closed, I knew that getting long-term financing was my number one priority. To secure financing on my terms, I had to do more than just manage the building.

I had two years to create value, to increase revenue, optimize the property's performance, and boost its appraisal value. My goal was simple: make the building worth more so that I could secure seventy-five percent financing at the new, higher valuation and take out the seller completely.

I renegotiated leases, improved tenant retention, increased rental income, and found ways to boost the property's cash flow. I added revenue streams, cut unnecessary costs, and ensured that when the banks reassessed the property, they would see a more profitable, more valuable asset. I wasn't just racing against time, I was racing against the seller, who was waiting for me to fail.

THE FINAL HOUR: SECURING THE MORTGAGE AT THE LAST POSSIBLE MOMENT

I spent two years going from bank to bank, trying to secure financing. I was young, and I didn't have the experience that lenders wanted for a deal of this size. They kept turning me down.

I tried everything. Managed the property myself. Worked my connections. Did everything in my power to prove that I could run this building successfully. Still, no mortgage approval.

The closer I got to the deadline, the more stressed I became. Then, on the very day his team was set to step in, ready to take back the building, I secured my financing. Laurentian Bank came through for me at the last possible moment.

I remember walking up to Mr. Jagermiester that day, looking him in the eye, and saying, "I'm sorry, but I'm paying you out. Leave the premises now." He didn't say a word. He just turned around and left. I had won.

I have owned that medical plaza ever since. It has been one of my most valuable assets, and over the years, I have redeveloped it, repositioned it, and transformed it into a property worth far beyond what I originally paid.

This deal saved me multiple times over the years. It all came down to a bet. A bet that I wouldn't fail. That's why I love real estate. When you play it right, you win big!

BETTING ON MYSELF WHEN NO ONE ELSE WOULD

Mr. Jagermiester was convinced I would fail. He structured the deal knowing that the odds were stacked against me, confident that in two years, I wouldn't be able to secure financing, and he would take the building back, along with every dollar I had invested.

What he didn't account for was my relentlessness.

For two years, I pushed, I strategized, and I worked every angle I could to increase the building's revenue and its appraised value. I knew that if I could prove the building was worth more than what I paid, I could leverage that increase to secure seventy-five percent financing at a higher valuation and remove him from the equation forever.

Every time a bank turned me down, I knocked on another door. Every time someone said "You can't do this," I worked harder to prove them wrong. Then, on the very last day, Laurentian Bank called. The mortgage was approved.

That moment changed me. It wasn't just about winning the deal, it was about proving that when I bet on myself, I don't lose.

My plan for this property was never just to buy and hold. From the very beginning, I saw so much more potential in it than just a medical plaza. I envisioned redeveloping it completely, turning it into something much bigger, much more valuable. It took time, patience, and the right moment to bring that vision to life.

It only took me twenty years, but today, that vision is finally becoming a reality. I severed off 1.6 acres, and we just completed the construction of an eighty-six unit multifamily building with 13,000 square feet of commercial space.

That's just Phase One. Phase Two will be even bigger, 300 multifamily units with 15,000 square feet of commercial on the main level. The best part? There could still be a Phase Three.

This property, once just a medical plaza, has become one of the most renowned medical centers in Kitchener. The tenant mix is strong, the demand is there, and the opportunities for further expansion keep growing. This deal wasn't just about buying a building. It was about seeing beyond what's there today and imagining what it could become tomorrow.

What this deal taught me is that in real estate, timing is everything. Some deals you flip in a year. Some deals take twenty years to reach their full potential. If you have a strong vision, if you see what others don't, and if you play the long game, real estate will always reward you.

THE VISION THAT TOOK TWENTY YEARS TO BUILD

When I first saw the medical plaza, I didn't just see a collection of doctors' offices and fast-food tenants. I saw a future development site.

I knew from the moment I bought it that this wasn't going to stay a medical plaza forever. Back then, I was just fighting to keep the deal together, to stop the seller from taking it back, to make sure the building stayed profitable. Redevelopment was a dream, but it wasn't something I could do right away.

Years passed, and the property did exactly what I needed it to do. It grew in value, generated income, and gave me the leverage I needed for future deals. That vision of what it *could* become never left my mind. Then, finally, the moment came.

Looking back, I realize that some of the best deals aren't the ones you flip quickly for a fast profit. They're the ones you nurture, develop, and expand over time, that require vision, patience, and execution. This property, which started as an ambitious bet, became one of the most valuable assets in my portfolio. After all these years, I'm still not done with it.

In real estate, the best deals never truly end. In the next chapter, I'll show you exactly why having the right funding can be the difference between winning and losing the game.

12

THE POWER OF
PRIVATE FUNDING
FAST, FLEXIBLE, AND GAME-CHANGING

Private money has been one of the most powerful tools in my real estate career. It has allowed me to move quickly, secure deals that others couldn't and build wealth in a way that traditional financing never could. While many investors automatically turn to banks for financing, I have always relied on private funding first.

Private lending is a game-changer because it allows me to move quickly, secure deals, and avoid the frustrating delays that come with institutional financing. Banks and traditional lenders are great for long-term stability, but in the fast-paced world of real estate, speed is everything.

Institutional financing, while beneficial in the long run, is slow. A bank mortgage can take thirty, sixty, ninety, or even one hundred and twenty days to finalize. In a competitive market, that's an eternity. Private money, on the other hand, can be secured within a week, sometimes even in a matter of days. When you find a deal that requires immediate action, waiting for a bank is simply not an option.

I have had clients call me in a panic, saying they needed hundreds of thousands of dollars overnight to close a deal. My response is always the same. "We can certainly help however it is going to be expensive." Private money is expensive, but what it gives you is the ability to move first, negotiate better, and win deals that others can't. In real estate, the person who has cash in hand almost always wins the deal. You need to look at the costs and confirm that paying the higher interest and fees can be made up by the discount on the purchase.

There are many reasons why a buyer might need to close immediately. Some try to secure bank financing, only to be declined at the last minute. Others firm up on deals without having financing in place and suddenly find themselves scrambling to avoid losing their deposit. Then there are the situations where a seller is desperate to sell, and the buyer who can bring cash to the table first walks away with the deal. In all of these cases, private funding is the solution.

Private money is also a powerful negotiation tool. If a seller needs to sell quickly, whether it's due to financial distress, a divorce, or any other pressing reason—a buyer who comes in with private funding has a huge advantage. When I walk into a deal with private money, I know I am in the strongest position possible. It gives me leverage to negotiate better terms, secure a lower purchase price, and make the deal work in my favor.

Private lenders are individuals who have money sitting in a bank account, a line of credit, or in registered funds, and they are looking for a solid return on their capital. Instead of letting their money sit idle, they put it to work in private mortgages, earning high-interest returns while using real estate as collateral.

There are all types of private lenders. Some are large companies that lend out hundreds of millions of dollars every year. Others are individual investors who have accumulated wealth and now prefer lending over managing properties, or working for a living. I know many investors who have transitioned from active real estate investing to private lending. They no longer want to deal with tenants or maintenance, so they lend money and collect interest every month. It's a smart way to generate long-term, passive wealth.

Private money is not just for investors who are buying properties. It is also used by developers and business owners who need short-term funding while they are waiting for bank approvals, zoning changes, or other regulatory approvals.

Private lending is not regulated by the banking system, there is a lot more flexibility, but that comes at a price. If a bank is offering a mortgage at five or six percent, private money will likely be at ten to twelve percent, sometimes more. Borrowers also need to factor in additional fees, including a lender fee and a broker fee. Typically, a borrower will pay two percent to the lender and one percent to the mortgage broker facilitating the deal.

All private lending transactions must go through a lawyer to ensure everything is properly registered on title. Even if you are borrowing from a family member, the loan should be structured legally to protect both parties. If it is done correctly, private lending is a safe, secured way to borrow and invest money.

When structuring a private loan, the most important factor is the loan-to-value ratio. This is based on either the appraised value or the purchase price of the property. Unlike banks, which will only lend on the lower of the two, private lenders often lend based on the appraised value. If you are buying a property for a million dollars, but the appraisal comes in at one point three million, there is a good chance that a private lender will lend based on the higher valuation.

The appraisal must be done by the private lender's appraiser, not the borrowers. Lenders want to ensure the valuation is accurate and fair, and they don't allow borrowers to stretch the numbers. This protects the lender and ensures the deal is being structured properly.

Private money has always been my go-to strategy. I use it to buy properties quickly, increase their value, and refinance with a bank once the deal is stabilized. This allows me to grow my portfolio without waiting on slow institutional financing. If I find a multifamily building that has significant upside. Whether it needs renovations, better management, or higher rents—private money gives me the ability to acquire it first, fix it up, and then refinance at a higher value.

Private lending is not just beneficial for borrowers; it's also an incredible opportunity for investors looking for passive income. Many investors transition into private lending after years of owning real estate. The returns can be significantly higher than traditional investments, and because the loans are secured by real estate, the risk is relatively low. Mortgage lending is typically structured as a twelve month investment, offering great returns compared to traditional savings or fixed-income investments. However, while the returns can be lucrative, investors need to understand that there can be delays in repayment, and if the funds are earmarked for something else on a strict timeline, it may not be the right investment choice.

Private mortgages provide short-term financing solutions to borrowers who need flexibility that banks cannot offer. These loans are often used for bridge financing, construction loans, land acquisitions, or distressed property purchases, all of which come with variables that can affect the exit timeline.

A borrower might intend to refinance with a bank at the end of the twelve month term, but if market conditions change, interest rates rise, or lending policies tighten, that exit strategy might be delayed. A sale that was expected to close might get pushed back. A construction project could face permitting issues or unexpected cost overruns. These are all real risks that investors need to be aware of.

A smart investor understands that real estate is not a liquid investment. While the borrower is legally obligated to repay, enforcing repayment takes time if an extension is needed or if legal action becomes necessary. Having a buffer period beyond the initial twelve month term ensures that you are not caught in a situation where your funds are tied up when you need them most.

When structured correctly, private mortgage lending offers consistent, high returns with real estate-backed security. However, like any investment, it requires understanding the risks, having a contingency plan, and ensuring the capital being invested is truly available for the duration of the deal, even if there are delays.

Private lending is an incredibly lucrative investment strategy, and after being in the business for twenty-five years, I can confidently say that the returns are both significant and passive. It has become one of the most stable and rewarding ways to grow wealth, and for many investors, it is an ideal retirement strategy.

Unlike active real estate investing, where you are dealing with tenants, property management, renovations, and market fluctuations, private lending offers steady monthly income without the headaches of property ownership. It allows investors to generate high returns while maintaining a hands-off approach.

Many of the wealthiest investors I know have transitioned from owning physical real estate to private mortgage lending as they approached retirement. They no longer want to deal with the stress of managing properties, yet they still want their capital working for them.

The appeal of private lending is simple:

- High, consistent returns—Interest rates on private mortgages are significantly higher than what traditional savings accounts, GICs, or bonds offer.
- Passive income—Instead of actively managing properties, lenders receive monthly interest payments while their capital is secured against real estate.
- Security—Private mortgages are backed by real estate, meaning there is tangible collateral in place.
- Flexibility—Lenders can choose their level of involvement, their risk tolerance, and the types of deals they want to finance.

For retirees or investors looking for predictable cash flow, private lending provides a stable income stream without the unpredictability of market-driven investments.

Private lenders typically earn seven to twelve percent annually on their capital, making it a much more attractive option than leaving money in a bank account earning next to nothing. This is why private lending has become such a major industry worldwide.

The principles of private lending apply across the globe. In the United States, private lenders, often called hard money lenders, play a critical role in financing fix-and-flip projects, multifamily acquisitions, and new developments. In Europe, private lending is often structured through boutique investment firms that cater to high-net-worth individuals. In Latin America and Southeast Asia, private lending is frequently arranged through personal networks, with investors lending to developers in exchange for high-interest returns.

Regardless of the country, the fundamentals remain the same. Private money is fast, flexible, and more expensive than traditional financing, but it gives borrowers access to capital when they need it most. For investors who understand how to use private funding correctly, it can be a game-changer.

Private funding is not just a financing tool—it's a strategic advantage. It provides the ability to get in, create value, and refinance with long-term financing. For those who transition into private lending, it becomes a way to create passive wealth, generating income without the work of managing properties.

If you want to be successful in real estate, you need to understand how to use private money. In the world of real estate investing, cash isn't just king . . . speed is.

THE BURLINGTON DEAL: A LESSON IN SPEED, STRATEGY, AND PRIVATE MONEY

One of my favorite deals was a multi-family acquisition in Burlington, Ontario. Not just because of the numbers, but because of how it all came together, fast, aggressive, and executed perfectly. This deal also meant a lot to me personally because I did it with my son Jacob.

It all started when two apartment buildings came onto the market, right next to a building we already owned. That alone made it an instant must-buy for me. When you own multiple buildings in the same area, you create efficiencies, and efficiencies create more profit.

This was not going to be a deal where we waited for financing approvals, drafted conditions, and took our time negotiating. I knew that if we didn't go in firm without conditions, someone else would scoop it up.

So, we did something bold. We put in a firm offer, with no conditions, and as a cash offer. This was an aggressive move, but I was confident in what we were buying. We knew the area, we knew the buildings, and we were comfortable with the risk. I don't recommend this to everyone. If you're not experienced or don't fully understand the building and its potential, a firm offer can be very risky.

We used private money to close the purchase quickly. The appraisal came in much higher than what we paid, around $500,000 to $600,000 more. This meant we were able to borrow against the appraised value, not just the purchase price, giving us even more leverage.

After closing, we immediately started working on securing institutional financing. The property qualified for an insured mortgage, which meant we could transition into a long-term bank loan at a much lower interest rate.

Right now, there are major incentives for multifamily investors who are creating new rental housing, reducing energy use, or improving buildings for long-term sustainability. The government has programs where you can secure up to a fifty year amortized mortgage with ninety-five percent financing for multifamily properties.

Within six months, we refinanced, paid off the private lender, and effectively owned the building with full bank financing.

THE REALITY OF BORROWING PRIVATE MONEY

Private money is not long-term financing. It's there to help you close deals fast, but you need to have an exit plan.

Most private mortgages are structured for twelve months, which means they are short-term loans. What many people don't realize is that some lenders lock you in for the full year, meaning that even if you refinance early, you still owe the full year's worth of interest.

I have seen many investors get caught up in this trap. They take out a private mortgage, thinking they'll refinance in six months, only to realize they are locked in for the full term and have to pay interest on the entire year, even if they don't need the loan anymore.

This is why I always make sure the private mortgages I take are open, or at least allow early payout after three months. It's critical to read the fine print and negotiate for flexibility when using private lenders.

I still use private money today, but I use it strategically. I know it's expensive, and I don't let it eat away at my equity. Private money is one of the most powerful tools in my real estate playbook.

I have used private funding for deals where the property had too many vacancies for a bank to finance it, when there was huge upside potential such as severing land, adding additional units, or increasing rents, and when the market was so hot that I had to close fast to win the deal.

Institutional financing takes time. If you need an insured mortgage, expect an even longer wait. With private money, you can close within a week, sometimes even in a matter of days. The truth is, sometimes time is worth more than the interest rate.

Say someone needs a million dollars in private money. The role of a mortgage broker is crucial here because they have access to private lenders. If you're an investor buying real estate, it's important to work with a broker who has access to private capital because private financing is a major part of the industry. It doesn't matter where you are, whether you're in Italy, Florida, or Canada, it is incredibly valuable to have access to people with deep pockets.

The cost of a million-dollar private mortgage depends on something called loan-to-value, which is based on the appraised value or the purchase price of the property. With private money, lenders may allow you to borrow against the appraised value rather than the purchase price.

For example, if you're buying a property for a million dollars but the appraisal comes in at 1.3 million, there's a chance the private lender will lend based on the higher appraised value. This is a key difference from institutional lenders, which typically base their loan amount on the lower of the purchase price or appraised value.

Let's talk about cost. You're paying ten, eleven, or twelve percent interest. Then you have your lender fee and broker fee, which add another four percent. If you do the math on that, it's not cheap, but if you've found an opportunity well below market value, the cost of private money is negligible compared to the profit you stand to make.

A lot of people in this business get caught up in the small costs. They focus too much on the lender fees, broker fees, or interest rates and lose sight of the bigger picture. Yes, you should always be detailed in your calculations, but don't nickel and dime the deal. If you step back and assess the overall opportunity, you'll see that the cost of private money is simply a tool.

For me, private money is my go-to strategy. It's my key to success, and it's what I always use. Once I've stabilized my property, increased its value, and positioned it for long-term growth, I refinance with a bank at a lower interest rate.

EXECUTING THE PRIVATE MONEY STRATEGY CORRECTLY

The biggest mistake I see new investors make is staying in private money too long. Private money is meant to help you move fast, but the cost adds up quickly.

In the 1970s, private lending wasn't a bad deal because mortgage rates were much higher. Today, when you can get CMHC-insured financing at three to four percent, it doesn't make sense to stay in a twelve percent private loan longer than necessary.

Private loans are interest-only, meaning you are never paying down the principal. That's why private money is not meant for long-term holds. For investors who can't qualify for a bank mortgage, private lending is sometimes the only option. Even if you have bad credit, irregular income, or outstanding taxes, private lenders will still finance you as long as the property taxes are up to date. This means that even if you can't go to the bank right now, you can still invest and build wealth using private money.

LOYALTY IN PRIVATE LENDING: WHY IT PAYS TO HAVE THE RIGHT RELATIONSHIPS

Private money is a relationship business. I have worked with some of the same private lenders for over twenty years. These relationships are built on trust, consistency, and fairness. Many investors make the mistake of shopping around for the lowest possible rate, thinking they can save a few thousand dollars. What they don't realize is that when you build loyalty with a lender, they will always be there for you when you need them.

If one of my long-time clients calls me and says, "Carmen, I have to close this deal tomorrow. Can you help me?" I'll make it happen for them. They won't question my fees because they know I deliver when it matters most.

BRRRR STRATEGY AND PRIVATE MONEY

The BRRRR strategy—Buy, Renovate, Rent, Refinance, Repeat—has become extremely popular, and private money is perfectly suited for it.

With private funding, you can buy a property, renovate it quickly, get tenants in, and then refinance with a bank to pay off the private loan. This allows you to build a portfolio much faster than if you relied solely on bank financing from the start.

AVOIDING THE BIGGEST PRIVATE MONEY MISTAKES

One of the biggest mistakes investors make is borrowing too much private money without a clear exit strategy. I have seen investors get into trouble by taking on too many properties at once, thinking they can refinance quickly, only to find out the market shifted or interest rates increased.

This is why it's so important to:

- Make sure your appraisals are realistic. Don't rely on inflated numbers.
- Have a defined exit strategy. Know exactly how you will refinance or sell.
- Keep your timeline in check. Don't hold private money longer than you need to.

PRIVATE MONEY AS A TOOL FOR SUCCESS

I have borrowed, repaid, and re-borrowed private loans more times than I can count. It has given me the speed and flexibility to scale my business and win deals that others couldn't.

The key is knowing when to use private money, how to structure the terms, and, most importantly, when to exit. When used correctly, private lending is one of the most powerful tools in real estate. It gives you buying power, negotiation leverage, and the ability to close deals fast.

It's important to be strategic, to scale smartly, and to avoid over-leveraging. Buying five hundred properties at once might sound like a great plan in theory, but in reality, it's a disaster waiting to happen. Growth should be methodical and calculated. Taking on multiple deals at the same time can work if you have the right team in place, but focus is key.

Private lenders each have their own set of criteria, and not all of them have the borrower's best interest in mind. Some lenders are what we call loan-to-own lenders. Individuals or firms that fund high-risk deals with the intent of taking over the property if the borrower defaults. These lenders charge high interest rates, sometimes as much as fifteen to eighteen percent, and they are not interested in helping borrowers succeed. They are looking for opportunities to take over distressed assets.

On the other hand, there are private lenders who work with investors to help them succeed. They focus on strong credit profiles, experience, and property value. Unlike banks, they don't require borrowers to fit a rigid mold. Instead, they take a common-sense approach. Assessing the borrower's experience, assets, and ability to execute the deal. If a borrower is new to real estate investing, lenders will often require additional security, such as cross-collateralizing another property or ensuring the deal has sufficient equity.

Lenders evaluate the deal from every angle. Where is the property located? What happens if the borrower stops making payments? Can the lender easily sell the property if needed? The more risk involved, the higher the cost of borrowing.

Market conditions, location, and the type of real estate also play a major role in private lending decisions. Exit strategy is key. Lenders want to know how the borrower plans to repay the loan. Will they refinance with a bank? Will they sell the property? Borrowers who don't have a clear plan for repayment often struggle when their term ends, and they find themselves unable to transition out of private financing.

When banks tighten their lending criteria, private money often becomes even more valuable. There are periods when banks reduce loan approvals, impose stricter stress test requirements, or limit the number of properties an investor can own. During these times, more investors turn to private capital to bridge the gap and continue expanding their portfolios.

When buying a property, it's critical to ensure that the appraised value is realistic. Some investors chase appraisers who will inflate valuations just to make a deal work, but that's a short-sighted approach that can lead to disaster. Doing the math honestly, understanding the numbers, and being conservative with projections is the only way to ensure long-term success.

Refinancing out of private money requires the right strategy. Mortgage brokers can be a huge asset because they have access to dozens, sometimes hundreds, of different lenders. A good broker will know exactly which lenders to approach first to get the best terms. If a deal gets declined by one institution, they can quickly pivot to another.

There's always a place for private lending, whether through institutional lenders, credit unions, mortgage investment corporations, or trust companies. Borrowers should never assume that a bank is their only option.

Due diligence is essential when working with private lenders. The lender will require an appraisal, and it must be done by an appraiser approved by them or their brokerage. Too many investors get caught ordering their own appraisals, only to find out later that the lender doesn't accept them. When buying a property, there will also be a site visit to confirm the asset is physically there.

The most critical part of borrowing private money is having a well-defined exit strategy. Borrowers need to know exactly how they will pay off the loan before they even sign the agreement. If the exit strategy is refinancing with a bank, they need to be sure they can qualify for that financing. If the exit strategy is selling the property, they need to be realistic about market conditions. If a sale takes longer than expected, they could end up carrying the private loan longer than planned, which can eat away at profits.

When working with a mortgage broker, I always ask upfront whether my client will qualify for a takeout mortgage. If the broker tells me they can secure financing when the private loan is up, I feel confident moving forward. The key is making sure the lender knows there is an exit plan.

In real estate, speed matters. Private money allows investors to move quickly, close deals fast, and create opportunities that wouldn't exist otherwise. It's a tool, not a crutch. If used correctly, it's one of the most powerful financing strategies available. If misused, it can be one of the quickest ways to lose money.

That's the balance of real estate investing. Knowing when to push forward and knowing when to step back. The best investors master that balance.

13

THE ART OF FINDING DEALS
UNLOCKING HIDDEN OPPORTUNITIES IN REAL ESTATE ACROSS NORTH AMERICA AND BEYOND

Finding the right deal in real estate isn't just about searching MLS listings or waiting for a property to fall into your lap. The most successful investors, whether they are in Canada, the U.S., or anywhere else in the world, know that the best deals are often hidden. They require research, persistence, networking, and a deep understanding of market conditions.

Real estate markets vary dramatically from country to country, and even within cities. The fundamentals of finding great deals remain the same worldwide. If you learn how to analyze a market, connect with key players, and structure your deals the right way, you can invest successfully anywhere.

Let's explore the global strategies for finding real estate deals, the differences between North America and international markets, and how you can take advantage of opportunities regardless of where you invest.

FINDING OFF-MARKET DEALS IN NORTH AMERICA

In North America, MLS (Multiple Listing Service) systems dominate the real estate industry. While they provide a convenient way to find available properties, the reality is that by the time a deal hits the MLS, it has already been seen, assessed, and potentially bid on by multiple investors. The real money is made by finding properties before they are listed.

Some of the most effective ways to find deals in Canada and the U.S. include:

1. Direct-to-Owner Marketing—Contacting property owners directly through letters, calls, or networking. In places like the U.S., investors use driving for dollars, where they physically drive around neighborhoods, looking for distressed properties that may have motivated sellers.

2. Real Estate Auctions—Many cities across North America hold property tax auctions where investors can buy distressed or foreclosed properties for below-market prices.

3. Wholesalers and Off-Market Brokers—Real estate wholesalers specialize in finding off-market deals

and assigning contracts to investors. In cities like Los Angeles, Miami, and Toronto, many high-value properties never hit the public market because they are traded within private networks.

4. Legal and Estate Sales—Connecting with estate attorneys, divorce lawyers, and bankruptcy trustees can give you access to properties before they are publicly listed.

5. Commercial Real Estate Networks—In commercial real estate, brokers often privately market properties to select investors before listing them online. Having relationships with these brokers is key.

HOW FINDING DEALS WORKS IN INTERNATIONAL MARKETS

Outside of North America, the real estate market operates very differently. In many countries, there is no centralized listing service like the MLS, and transactions are far more relationship-driven.

In Europe, many high-end properties are sold through private networks rather than public listings. In France, Italy, and Spain, some of the best real estate never even hits the open market. Instead, agents work with select buyers behind the scenes. This means that in international investing, having the right contacts is everything.

In Latin America, such as Mexico, Costa Rica, and Colombia, many properties are sold directly by owners. There is less reliance on brokers, and investors often find deals by building relationships with local sellers. In these markets, being physically present and networking is the best way to find opportunities.

In Southeast Asia, particularly in countries like Thailand and the Philippines, foreigners often have restrictions on buying land, but they can own condominium units. Many investors find deals by working with expat communities and using social media groups dedicated to real estate investments.

The Middle East, particularly Dubai, has seen explosive real estate growth, with many off-market transactions happening through private developer connections. Some of the most lucrative deals come from buying pre-construction units from developers before they hit the public market.

Each market has its own set of rules, regulations, and cultural nuances, but the fundamental principles remain the same:

- Get to know the market before investing.
- Build relationships with the key players.
- Find off-market opportunities through direct outreach and networking.

USING TECHNOLOGY TO FIND DEALS WORLDWIDE

Technology has changed the way investors find deals. In North America and globally, investors are now leveraging big data, AI, and automation to identify opportunities before others.

Some of the most effective tools used to find deals today include:

- PropStream (U.S.)—A powerful data platform that allows investors to find distressed properties, absentee owners, and motivated sellers.
- CoStar (North America & Europe)—One of the most comprehensive commercial real estate databases, used by institutional investors to track properties.
- Zillow & Redfin (U.S.), Realtor.ca (Canada), and Rightmove (UK)—While public listings are not always the best deals, these platforms provide valuable market insights.
- AirDNA (Global)—Essential for investors looking to buy short-term rental properties, providing data on Airbnb performance worldwide.
- LinkedIn & Facebook Real Estate Groups—Many international real estate deals happen within private online communities.

By combining traditional deal-finding strategies with modern data tools, investors can now track, analyze, and act on opportunities faster than ever before.

HOW TO SPOT A GREAT DEAL—
ANYWHERE IN THE WORLD

Whether you are investing in Canada, the U.S., Europe, or Asia, there are key indicators that help identify a great deal.

The first step is understanding if the market is growing or declining. Looking at population growth, job creation, and infrastructure investment can tell you whether a location is rising in value or stagnating.

The second step is looking at income vs. expenses. If the cash flow is strong and the property is in a market with upside potential, it is worth pursuing.

In high-demand areas like New York, London, or Vancouver, cap rates tend to be lower because investors are banking on appreciation. In emerging markets like Mexico, Eastern Europe, or parts of Africa, cap rates are often much higher because investors want higher cash flow to offset the risk.

If a property offers significant upside potential, whether through renovation, higher rents, or added density, it becomes an even stronger investment.

MASTERING THE ART OF FINDING DEALS

The process of finding deals in real estate is both an art and a science.

It requires a combination of market research, relationship-building, financial analysis, and sometimes just being in the right place at the right time.

If you are investing in North America, the best deals are often found off-market—before they hit the MLS. If you are looking internationally, you need to understand how real estate is transacted in that specific market.

The key takeaway is that great deals don't come to you, you go out and find them.

Once you master the ability to source and analyze properties, you will never have to worry about finding the next opportunity. You will know exactly where to look, who to talk to, and how to act before anyone else does.

THE HUNT FOR OFF-MARKET DEALS

Some of the best deals I have ever secured came from simply paying attention. Driving through neighborhoods, noticing buildings that looked like they had potential, and then tracking down the owner.

There are so many tools today that allow you to track down ownership records. Some apps and online platforms can tell you exactly who owns a property, what they paid for it, and whether there's a mortgage on it. Once you have that information, it is a matter of reaching out, starting a conversation, and seeing if there is an opportunity to buy.

If you see an apartment building that catches your eye, or a six-unit or twelve-unit property that looks like it could use some work, that's a potential opportunity. It may be a distressed asset where the owner is struggling to keep up with maintenance. Or it may be a long-time landlord who is finally ready to sell but hasn't yet listed the property.

I have personally bought properties by knocking on doors, making calls, and sending letters. There have been deals where the seller wasn't even thinking about selling until I presented an offer that made sense for them.

One way to find hidden deals is through law firms and accounting firms that specialize in real estate transactions. These professionals often work with clients who are looking to sell their properties, whether for tax reasons, estate planning, or restructuring their portfolio.

If you can build relationships with these professionals, you can get access to deals before they ever hit the market. Many times, sellers do not want to list their properties publicly, they would rather sell quietly to the right buyer. If you position yourself as a serious, ready-to-close investor, you can tap into these exclusive opportunities.

Another strategy is working closely with real estate agents, but not in the way you might think. Most agents aren't calling just anyone when they get a hot deal. They are calling their top investors first. If you want to be on that list, you need to build relationships with agents who specialize in multifamily and commercial deals so they think of you before listing a property publicly.

Sometimes, a real estate agent will get a listing from a friend or family member who isn't familiar with the market value, and that's when you can find a hidden gem. The moment you hear about the deal, you need to be ready to jump on it before the rest of the world finds out.

FINDING THE UPSIDE:
THE SECRET TO VALUE CREATION

A property's value is not just based on what it is today, but on what it could become.

If a building has below-market rents, that's an opportunity. You might not be able to increase those rents immediately, but over time, as tenants turn over, you can bring rents up to market rates and significantly increase the property's value.

A fully stabilized building, where every unit is at market rent and all value has already been created, is not as attractive to investors.

Vacancies, on the other hand, can be a golden opportunity. If a property is half-vacant, you can immediately raise those rents to market levels and dramatically increase the value.

Sometimes, a property has extra land that can be severed or developed, adding even more value. If there's an unused basement, garage, or storage space, you can convert it into additional rental income.

REAL ESTATE IS A GAME OF STRATEGY

Finding a great deal isn't about luck. It's about strategy, research, and knowing what to look for. If you find the right deal, analyze the numbers correctly, and understand how to add value, you can turn a good deal into a great one.

If you skip the details, trust the wrong numbers, or fail to do your research, you could find yourself trapped in a bad investment with no way out.

14

PRIVATE BANKING, NOT THE BEST OPTION FOR REAL ESTATE INVESTORS

Private banking is often viewed as an exclusive privilege for high-net-worth individuals, promising tailored financial solutions, personalized service, and a streamlined approach to managing wealth. On the surface, it seems like an investor's dream, dedicated account managers, preferential treatment, and supposedly easier access to capital. When it comes to real estate financing, private banking can actually become a roadblock rather than an advantage.

At first, the experience was seamless. Your assigned banker takes care of everything, and the first few mortgages get approved quickly. They make you feel like you're part of an elite financial club, where money flows effortlessly, and access to funding is just a phone call away.

What most investors don't realize is that private banking is not designed for real estate investors.

The real purpose of private banking is to sell investment products. The institution wants your money tied up in their managed portfolios, funds, and wealth management products, not in real estate. The bankers are trained to encourage clients to put their money into the bank's financial instruments, not into properties.

The biggest problem arises when you go beyond your first few mortgages. That's when private banking starts to show its limitations. Unlike regular banking, where you can shop around and speak with different mortgage specialists, private banking locks you into working with one specific banker. That banker becomes your only point of contact.

If you are lucky and get an aggressive, real estate-savvy banker, you might be able to secure multiple mortgages with little resistance. If your banker is slow, inexperienced, or simply not motivated to fight for your deals, you are stuck. Even if you meet another mortgage specialist within the same institution who is willing to push your file through, they won't be able to help you because you are tied to private banking.

I was working with a phenomenal private banker who understood my business, processed my deals efficiently, and got things done fast. One day, she got transferred, and I was assigned to someone else. That's when everything changed. My new banker didn't understand real estate investing, wasn't willing to push for approvals, and wasn't nearly as proactive as my previous banker. Suddenly, my easy approvals became challenges, and simple deals turned into long, drawn-out struggles.

At the same time, I was introduced to a mortgage broker who worked outside of the bank but had deep connections within the same institution. He had a reputation for getting complex deals approved because he knew how to package them properly, how to present them to underwriters, and how to navigate the system. He called me one day with good news. "Carmen, I have an approval for you." Then he followed with, "There's a problem." I asked what it was, and he explained, "because you're in private banking, they won't let me submit the file."

This meant that even though my mortgage was already approved through the broker, the bank wouldn't process it because I was in private banking. Instead, I had to go back to my assigned banker, who declined the exact same deal.

I lost financing for a five-unit property, not because I wasn't qualified, not because the deal wasn't strong, but because of a bureaucratic policy that blocked me from working with someone else in the same institution. That was the moment I realized private banking wasn't the solution I thought it was.

I once worked with a banker in New Brunswick who approved construction financing for a twenty-four unit building in just three weeks. It was one of the smoothest transactions I had ever experienced, low rates, flexible draws, competitive terms. I was so impressed that I asked if he could handle a deal for me in Ontario.

He started working on it, and everything seemed to be moving forward. Then I got a call. "Sorry, we can't approve this financing. Your corporate account is managed by another department, and they have to handle it."

That was it. A banker who had just approved a multi-million dollar deal with ease was suddenly unable to process my Ontario file because of internal banking restrictions. That was the last time I ever did a deal with that institution.

Real estate financing isn't just about your finances or the property itself, it's about who is handling your file and how motivated they are to push it through. Two different bankers in the same institution can give you completely different answers. The same borrower, with the same portfolio, can get an approval from one banker and a rejection from another.

This is why mortgage brokers are so powerful. Unlike private bankers, mortgage brokers are not tied to just one institution. They have access to multiple lenders, allowing them to shop around and find the best financing for your situation. They know which lenders work best for investors, which underwriters are real estate-friendly, and which alternative lenders will approve deals that traditional banks won't.

A good mortgage broker is not just submitting an application—they are structuring the deal in a way that ensures approval.

In commercial mortgages, there are ways to structure financing for better terms. Most Bank financing can offer government-insured loans at lower interest rates, but the qualification process is strict. Lenders require a strong net worth, a track record of success, and a property that meets their guidelines. If an investor doesn't meet the requirements, they often have to turn to semi-private or alternative lenders, which charge higher rates but are easier to access.

Eventually, every investor hits a wall with financing or capital to scale the enterprise. When that happens, alternative strategies are needed to keep moving forward. That is where joint ventures come into play.

Real estate financing is a game of strategy. It's not just about having strong financials, it's about working with the right people, understanding how to structure deals, and knowing when to pivot to alternative solutions. The same borrower can get different answers depending on who they are dealing with, how the file is presented, and whether the banker or broker is motivated to get the deal done.

When traditional financing options run out, smart investors don't stop growing, they find another way. Joint ventures offer a way to leverage partnerships to keep scaling, even when financing becomes difficult or liquidity may be an issue. In the next chapter, I'll share exactly how I have structured joint ventures, the lessons I've learned, and how the right partnerships can help investors grow beyond what they thought was possible.

15

THE POWER OF
JOINT VENTURES
LEVERAGING PARTNERSHIPS TO SCALE

Every real estate investor reaches a point where capital becomes the biggest hurdle. It's not about the ability to find deals, manage properties, or secure financing. It's about scaling, about having enough funds to continue acquiring assets while keeping reserves for renovations, maintenance, and unexpected costs.

This is where joint ventures become one of the most powerful tools in real estate investing. It allows you to keep growing, even when your own capital is tied up. A strong joint venture means that two or more parties can combine their resources, their expertise, and their connections to take on larger deals, expand their portfolios, and ultimately create more wealth than they could alone.

For many investors, the first time they explore a joint venture is when they hit a personal financial ceiling.

Maybe they have maxed out their ability to get traditional mortgages, or perhaps they have reached a point where their own liquid funds are stretched too thin. Whatever the reason, they know they need to find another way to keep moving forward, and bringing in a partner with capital is often the best solution.

I have done many joint ventures, and each one has been structured to benefit both parties while allowing the deal to move forward. It is always about structuring the right arrangement, where each party's contributions and responsibilities are clearly defined. Joint ventures work because they allow each partner to focus on their strengths while relying on the other to cover what they cannot.

One of the most important lessons I have learned over the years is that a joint venture is only as good as the agreement behind it. Everything must be laid out in writing. A verbal agreement or a handshake deal may seem simple and efficient at first, but over time, as circumstances change, memories fade, and profits are on the line, problems can arise. I have entered into partnerships without proper documentation in the past, trusting that everyone was on the same page, and it cost me dearly. There were misunderstandings about profit splits, disagreements about responsibilities, and in some cases, outright conflicts that could have been avoided if we had put everything in writing.

When structuring a joint venture, it is critical to define the roles clearly. Typically, one partner brings the capital while the other is responsible for managing the deal. The capital partner provides the funds for the down payment, closing costs, and sometimes even renovation costs, while the active partner finds the deal, negotiates the purchase, handles tenant management, oversees renovations, and ensures the investment is profitable. This kind of arrangement works well because it allows an investor with capital to put their money to work without taking on the daily responsibilities of running a property, while the active partner benefits by being able to acquire assets they wouldn't have been able to afford alone.

Equity splits in joint ventures vary depending on the level of contribution from each party. If both partners are bringing equal amounts of capital and both are involved in operations, a 50/50 split makes sense. If one partner is putting up all the money and qualifying for the mortgage while the other partner is managing the deal, then the split is often more in favor of the capital provider. It could be 70/30 or 80/20, depending on how much work the active partner is doing and how much risk the capital partner is taking.

There are times when an active investor has the experience, the team, and the ability to manage multiple projects, but they simply don't have the funds to scale. This is when bringing in joint venture partners can allow for exponential growth.

I have structured joint ventures where the passive investor simply collects a return, while I handle everything from acquisition to management. I have also been in deals where my partner was involved in decision-making, bringing not only money but also experience and additional connections that helped strengthen the business.

One of the biggest risks in joint ventures is misalignment in expectations. Before entering into any partnership, there must be full transparency about what each person wants out of the deal. Some investors want to hold long-term, while others prefer short-term flips. Some want immediate cash flow, while others are focused on appreciation. If one partner is expecting a quick return while the other is thinking five or ten years down the road, conflicts will arise.

Trust is everything in a joint venture. Even with a solid contract, if you do not trust your partner, the business relationship will not last. A joint venture is like a marriage in the business world. You are committing to a financial and operational relationship that will last years, possibly even decades. If there are red flags early on, it is better to walk away before signing anything rather than dealing with a messy breakup down the line.

One of the best ways to protect both parties in a joint venture is to ensure that there is an agreed-upon exit strategy. What happens if one partner wants to sell, but the other doesn't? What if a partner passes away? What if market conditions change and refinancing isn't an option? These are scenarios that must be planned for before signing the agreement.

Joint ventures come in many forms. Some are structured as corporations where each partner owns shares. Others are agreements between individuals that outline the roles and responsibilities of each party. Some deals are structured with a profit participation agreement, where one partner has no direct ownership but is entitled to a share of the profits. The right structure depends on the nature of the deal, tax considerations, and each partner's level of involvement.

I have worked with investors who have built entire portfolios using joint ventures, never using their own money but instead leveraging partnerships to scale. They focused on finding the right deals, structuring agreements properly, and maintaining strong relationships with their partners.

Joint ventures work in any market condition. When the market is booming, they allow investors to pool capital and acquire larger deals. When financing becomes tight, joint ventures provide a way to keep buying properties without relying solely on one person's borrowing power.

I have personally used joint ventures to expand into new markets, take on bigger projects, and scale faster than I ever could have alone.

Real estate is not a solo game. The most successful investors are the ones who know how to structure partnerships, leverage relationships, and build long-term business connections.

Joint ventures aren't just about acquiring more properties. They are about building the right team, creating lasting partnerships, and structuring deals that allow everyone to win. When done correctly, they are one of the most powerful tools an investor can use to accelerate growth and build generational wealth.

Sometimes, silent partners aren't so silent, because it's *their* money. Make sure you know exactly who your silent partner is before you bring them into a deal. People's true colors come out when money is involved. I've seen it happen more times than I can count. Someone I considered a good friend, someone I had spent time with, laughed with, built trust with—suddenly became a completely different person when things didn't go exactly as expected. Nothing in business is ever guaranteed, and that applies to real estate as well. It's a weighted average over time, not a straight path of guaranteed success. I've seen people who were perfectly fine when everything was going well suddenly become aggressive, self-serving, and completely indifferent to the bigger picture the moment their money wasn't performing the way they expected.

In those moments, the focus shifts. It's no longer about the team, about the shared vision, or about the long-term potential. It becomes *all about them*. Their money. Their return. Even if you're in the trenches, even if you're the one doing all the work. They just want their money. That's why it's critical to partner with like-minded people who share your vision, your values, and your long-term outlook.

Before you take on an investment partner, take your time. Get to know them. See how they react to challenges. It's like dating before marriage, you don't commit until you've seen what they're really like in different situations. My mistake was thinking that years of friendship meant we would be good business partners.

Not every deal is going to be great. Real estate, like any other investment, has ups and downs. Even the most stable, well-structured investment can face unexpected challenges. Markets shift, regulations change, interest rates rise, tenants leave, renovations cost more than expected, there are always variables.

There are no guarantees in any investment. In my experience, real estate is one of the most stable and secure investment vehicles available. Even in the most challenging times, it holds value, and over the long run, it remains one of the most proven ways to build wealth.

That said, anyone coming into a real estate deal needs to understand that nothing is guaranteed. As the lead investor, you should always disclose risks upfront. Many people jump into partnerships full of excitement, focusing only on the positives. They draft contracts that outline all the ways they're going to win. The projected profits. The potential appreciation. The expected returns. Very few people sit down and seriously discuss, what if something goes wrong?

On one side, you could be investing with someone who isn't pulling their weight, leaving you to do all the work. On the other side, you could have a silent partner who suddenly decides they need their money back immediately. Maybe their kids are going to university, or they're buying a house, or they simply get nervous about the market. Now, six months before the agreed-upon timeline, they want out.

That's not how JV`s or equity investments work. Everyone involved needs to fully understand that real estate is a long-term game. I've had investors who, looking back, should have never been in real estate. These were people who, instead of using money they could afford to leave in the market, were investing funds they might need within a year or two. They didn't fully understand what they were getting into. When they suddenly wanted out early, it created stress, unnecessary complications, and in some cases, the potential to ruin a deal entirely.

I have learned to choose my partners wisely. To work with people who understand the business. To be upfront about risks and make sure that every investor knows exactly what they are getting into. In this business, the last thing you want is a silent partner who suddenly finds their voice, and turns your dream deal into a nightmare.

Real estate is a long-term game. It is not a get-rich-quick scheme, nor is it a liquid asset that you can just cash out whenever you feel like it. If an investor is in a financial position where they may need to pull their money out unexpectedly, they should not be tying up their capital in real estate.

A long-term real estate investment requires patience, stability, and a clear understanding that capital will be tied up for a period of time.

Shorter-term investments, such as flips, land development, pre-construction assignments, and bridge financing, can generate significant profits in a relatively short period. They also come with unpredictability. Market conditions can shift, buyers can back out, construction can be delayed, or refinancing options may not be available as planned.

This is why, even with short-term real estate deals, investors need to be prepared for flexibility. You may have an expected exit in twelve or eighteen months, but if the market slows down, if interest rates rise unexpectedly, or if your refinancing strategy falls through, that timeline could be pushed out. If an investor needs their money back at a specific time, that creates unnecessary pressure and potential financial strain.

A real estate investor must always have contingency plans. If the original exit doesn't work, is there an alternative? Can the property be rented out for cash flow until the market rebounds? Can the financing be extended? Are there other investors willing to step in and buy out a partner if necessary?

In real estate, flexibility is key. When things go according to plan, short-term deals can be incredibly lucrative. When things don't line up perfectly, patience and the ability to adjust are what separate successful investors from those who panic. The ones who truly understand the investment will ride the ups and downs with you, knowing that real estate is a long game. The ones who don't will panic, demand their money back, and potentially cause more problems than they solve.

THE CAUTIONARY TALE OF MR. SARDINE

Sometimes, the people who talk the biggest game deliver the least. I have always trusted my gut when it comes to deals, that Feel the Deal instinct that has guided me through some of the best investments of my career. Every now and then, even the most seasoned investor can get caught up in the illusion of opportunity, in the promise of something bigger than what they could achieve alone.

That's how I ended up in business with Mr. Sardine. He wasn't a silent partner, nor was he the one bringing the money to the table. We were the capital partners, and he was supposed to be the active one, the person making things happen. He sold us on a vision, big deals, major developers, powerful investors. He had the network, the influence, and the ability to unlock opportunities we otherwise wouldn't have access to. According to him, this partnership would be the beginning of something extraordinary.

I ignored that little voice in my head, the one that told me to take a step back and assess. I let myself want what he was selling, instead of trusting the instincts that had never steered me wrong before. Twelve months later, what did we have? Not a single deal. Not one investor. Not one major connection that led to anything meaningful.

What we did have was an over-promiser, an under-deliverer, and a walking disaster of a business relationship. The empire he promised never materialized. Instead, what I got was a sloppy, sardine-eating mess of a so-called partner who contributed absolutely nothing but wasted time and frustration. Then it got worse.

When it became clear that his promises were empty, instead of walking away, Mr. Sardine decided he would steal what he could from me and try to build my business as his own. He took my database, my staff, and copied my entire marketing strategy, believing that if he had my contacts, my systems, and my structure, he could replicate my success. He didn't understand one critical thing.

Success isn't about what you take, it's about what you create. He could steal my database, but he couldn't steal the relationships I built. He could copy my marketing, but he couldn't copy the trust and credibility I had earned over years in this business. He could try to recreate my strategy, but without the knowledge, the experience, and the actual ability to execute, he was nothing more than a bad imitation. In the end, he failed.

Real estate is a business of relationships and execution. You can't fake it. You can't talk your way into long-term success. You can't steal someone else's formula and expect the same results. The industry is full of big talkers. If you're not careful, if you don't vet your partners properly, you will end up wasting time, money, and energy on someone who was never capable of delivering in the first place.

The lesson I learned from Mr. Sardine? Trust your gut. Protect what you've built. Be generous, but don't give away your special sauce. Most importantly, never let words overshadow actions.

16

INVESTING PASSIVELY WITH SUCCESS

There are many ways to invest passively in real estate, allowing you to earn strong returns without the responsibilities of managing properties. Passive investing is a great option for those who want to build wealth without dealing with tenants, renovations, or property management.

There are multiple streams of passive investing. You could be a mortgage lender, where your money is loaned out through private mortgages, generating high-interest returns secured by real estate. You can invest with experienced developers, like myself, who do construction and large-scale development projects. Or you can invest in a Real Estate Investment Trust (REIT), which allows you to own a share of multiple properties without having to buy them individually.

A REIT is a structure that allows investors to pool their money together and invest in real estate without having to qualify for a mortgage or actively manage properties. A REIT is structured through a mutual fund trust, meaning you can invest using both registered funds (such as RRSPs, TFSAs, and LIRAs) or cash.

For example, District REIT, which is our REIT, allows investors to partner with us. Instead of going out and buying apartment buildings, commercial plazas, or other real estate assets on your own, you can buy units in the REIT and benefit from a diverse portfolio of income-generating properties.

One key distinction is that District REIT is a private REIT, meaning it is not traded on the stock market and is not affected by market volatility the way a public REIT is. Public REITs are subject to stock market fluctuations and investor sentiment, which can cause their prices to swing up and down, even when the underlying real estate assets remain strong. Private REITs, on the other hand, are directly tied to the value and income of the real estate itself, making them more stable and insulated from market turbulence.

Each REIT has its own minimum investment requirement. Ours, for example, starts at $10,000, and when you invest, you are purchasing units in the REIT, not stocks. Unlike stocks, where the value can fluctuate based on market sentiment, private REITs are backed by real, income-producing real estate assets, which provide stability and long-term appreciation. www.feelthedeal.com

One of the most attractive features of a REIT is the monthly distribution payments that investors receive. In the case of District REIT, investors receive an eight percent annual distribution, paid monthly. What makes this structure even more powerful is the tax efficiency of these payments.

The eight percent return that investors receive annually is classified as a return of capital, which means it is not taxed immediately. This makes it an extremely tax-advantageous product compared to traditional income-generating investments.

If you compare this to a mortgage investment, where you might be earning sixteen percent annually, that income is fully taxable. If you are in a fifty percent tax bracket (oh Canada), half of that return is lost to taxes. With a private REIT, because your distribution is not taxed as income, the after-tax benefits can be just as strong, if not better, than higher-yield mortgage investments.

Beyond the financial benefits, a REIT is also a hassle-free investment. You don't have to qualify for a mortgage, you don't have to deal with tenants, you don't have to manage a property, and you don't have to handle maintenance or renovations.

For many investors, private REITs offer a lower-risk, hands-off way to build long-term wealth while benefiting from the security and appreciation of stabilized real estate assets.

The beauty of a REIT is that it can continuously grow and expand, creating an ongoing cycle of investment and wealth-building. There's no limit to the number of units we can acquire. As we build the portfolio and raise more capital, the REIT grows in size, becoming a larger and larger opportunity for investors.

What makes this type of investment so powerful is that investors benefit from our expertise. Our team has decades of experience in real estate development, acquisitions, financing, and management. Instead of buying and managing properties on their own, investors in the REIT, partner with seasoned professionals who understand the market, execute deals efficiently, and create long-term value.

Another unique advantage of District REIT is that our sister company has multiple divisions. We build commercial, multi residential properties specifically for the REIT, meaning that District REIT has first access to brand-new, high-quality assets. Many of the properties within the REIT portfolio are newly developed buildings, which means lower maintenance costs, modern amenities, and higher tenant demand, all contributing to stronger long-term performance.

My partner, Richard, and I are both trustees and founders of the REIT, but we don't make decisions alone.

Every major acquisition or transaction goes through the Board of Directors, ensuring full transparency and accountability. Investors can feel confident knowing that experienced professionals are reviewing each decision, validating the numbers, and maintaining strong corporate governance.

This also means that there is no conflict of interest. Richard and I cannot simply buy a property, renovate it, and flip it to the REIT for a profit. The Board reviews all acquisitions, ensuring that every transaction meets strict investment criteria.

This low-risk investment structure provides investors with steady, consistent returns. Some years, like one particular year when property values surged, we achieved eighteen percent returns. On average, investors can expect fourteen to fifteen percent annual returns on their money, making it an incredibly strong and stable investment option.

For those investing through registered funds, such as RRSPs, TFSAs, or LIRAs, the growth is even more powerful. The returns are reinvested tax-free within the registered account, the investment compounds exponentially, creating long-term, tax-efficient wealth accumulation.

There is also something called a DRIP (Dividend Reinvestment Plan), which allows investors to automatically reinvest their distributions rather than taking them as cash. Instead of receiving the eight percent annual return in cash each month, investors can roll it into additional units, increasing their stake in the REIT. This means their investment compounds over time, generating returns on their returns.

By reinvesting distributions, investors benefit from accelerated growth, allowing their investment to scale much faster than if they were simply taking cash payouts. This is a powerful tool for those who are focused on long-term wealth accumulation, as it leverages the power of compound interest to exponentially increase returns. Investors receive quarterly statements outlining their holdings, making it an incredibly passive and hands-off investment strategy.

For those who prioritize cash flow but still want to stay in a lower-risk environment, investing in District REIT or a similar private REIT can be an excellent option. It provides steady income, stable asset-backed growth, and professional management.

One of the most important factors when investing in a REIT is understanding who is behind the scenes. Not all REITs are created equal, and the expertise of the management team makes a huge difference in performance. District REIT is a private REIT, which means it is not publicly traded on the stock exchange, and its value is based on real market conditions and property performance, rather than stock market fluctuations.

The ultimate goal of a private REIT is growth. Over time, there are several potential exit strategies that create major financial success for investors:

- Going public—When a private REIT reaches a significant size, typically $1 billion to $2 billion in assets, it may go public. This transition allows investors to liquidate their holdings at a much higher value, often leading to substantial gains.

- Selling the portfolio—A private REIT may be acquired by a larger institutional investor or merged into another real estate fund. When this happens, all investors in the REIT share in the profits from the sale.

- Continuing to scale privately—Some REITs remain private, continuing to expand their portfolio, increase cash flow, and grow investor returns while keeping a stable, non-market-driven valuation.

A private REIT like District REIT allows investors to be part of an evolving, growing business, where experienced professionals manage the assets, optimize returns, and scale the portfolio strategically.

THE STABILITY OF PRIVATE REITS AND LONG-TERM INVESTING

District REIT is a diversified private REIT, meaning it doesn't focus on just one type of real estate asset. It has the flexibility to invest in apartment buildings, industrial properties, commercial spaces, and even mortgage lending. This diversification helps balance the portfolio, reducing risk and ensuring stability even when market conditions shift.

Investing in a private REIT means that you're in a long-term vehicle that is actively managed by experienced professionals who understand the market and anticipate trends over the next five, ten, or even twenty years. Unlike public REITs, which can be highly liquid but vulnerable to stock market volatility, private REITs offer a more stable, long-term approach.

LIQUIDITY IN PRIVATE REITS

While a private REIT isn't as liquid as a public REIT, investors can redeem their units within a time frame that typically ranges from thirty to ninety days, depending on liquidity conditions at the time of redemption. There are no penalties for redeeming, but the process is slower than selling stocks on an exchange. However, this illiquidity is actually an advantage because it protects the fund from market panic and short-term speculation, which can drive down values in publicly traded REITs.

INVESTING IN SECONDARY MARKETS

District REIT is heavily focused on secondary markets, which have shown incredible growth over the years. Cities like London, Woodstock, and Kitchener have flourished, particularly when COVID hit, as people moved out of large urban centers in search of more space and affordability. These regions continue to grow, as housing demand remains high, making them ideal for long-term real estate investment.

MULTIFAMILY AND ESSENTIAL-USE PROPERTIES: THE SMARTEST INVESTMENT SECTORS

With the ongoing housing crisis, multifamily properties are one of the best places to invest. People will always need a place to live, and demand for rental housing continues to grow, making multifamily real estate a stable and recession-resistant investment.

Another highly stable investment class is essential-use properties. Assets that people rely on daily, such as medical buildings, grocery stores, pharmacies, and liquor stores. These businesses are necessities and are far less vulnerable to economic downturns.

WHY PRIVATE REITS ARE IDEAL FOR RETIREMENT INVESTORS

District REIT has many senior investors who use their registered funds (RRSPs, TFSAs, and LIRAs) to generate passive income in retirement. Many retirees require a certain amount of income each year but don't want to eat into their principal investment.

The DRIP (Dividend Reinvestment Plan) allows them to reinvest their distributions, keeping their investment growing while still receiving the income they need. This way, their capital remains intact while still generating a consistent return.

17

THE REALITY OF LONG-TERM INVESTMENTS AND MARKET DISRUPTIONS

Investing in real estate development projects often requires a five-to-seven-year commitment, and investors need to be prepared for market fluctuations. For example, COVID-19 was a perfect example of an unpredictable global event that impacted the entire industry.

The pandemic shut down construction and development for over two years, leading to supply chain issues, labor shortages, and financing difficulties. As a result, costs skyrocketed, making it impossible for builders to accurately project budgets, which in turn affected financing and timelines.

UNDERSTANDING LIMITED PARTNERSHIPS AND DEVELOPMENT INVESTMENTS

Earlier in this book, I shared the story of a property in Kitchener, where I sat across the table from a shrewd German businessman who couldn't wait to take the deal away from me. That same property, years later, became one of our major development projects. We recently completed five rental units on one of the phases, and today, we are working on a 262-unit development on that very same site.

When investors look to get involved in these types of opportunities, they typically partner with an established company, one with years of experience, a strong track record, and a team that knows how to execute projects successfully. It's not just about the numbers. You need to know who is behind the deal.

When an investor participates in a development project, they receive a full package from the company outlining every detail of the project:

- Appraisals
- Current development stages
- Projected timelines
- Income potential
- Market analysis

Every single nook and cranny of the deal is laid out, allowing investors to evaluate the opportunity with full transparency.

One of the most common ways to invest in real estate development is through a Limited Partnership (LP). A limited partnership is structured so that investors contribute capital to a project while the general partner (the developer or investment firm) manages and executes the project. Investors in an LP typically receive a percentage of profits without having to be involved in the day-to-day operations.

The example of the Kitchener project is a single-property limited partnership, where the targeted return is twenty-seven percent per year. What makes this particular investment appealing is that it is purpose-built rental combined with medical-use spaces. These two high-demand sectors offer incredible stability, even in challenging market conditions.

- Purpose-built rental housing is one of the strongest real estate investments today due to the ongoing housing crisis.
- Medical facilities, such as clinics, dental offices, and healthcare centers are necessity-driven businesses that provide reliable income streams.

With multi-unit residential buildings, you have hundreds of tenants paying the mortgage, not just one or two. This spreads the risk across multiple income sources, making it a safer and more predictable investment.

INVESTMENT MINIMUMS AND REGULATIONS

Typically, the minimum investment for a limited partnership is $150,000. However, District REIT, which is a more accessible investment vehicle, has a minimum investment of $10,000, making it available to a broader range of investors.

Securities regulators in Canada and the U.S. strictly regulate REITs, limited partnerships, and other real estate investment funds.

For REITs like District REIT, anyone can invest, but regulations limit how much you are allowed to invest annually to protect investors.

For limited partnerships and development projects, the investment opportunities are typically geared toward accredited investors.

UNDERSTANDING TIMELINES
AND PROJECT RISKS

Every development project comes with a timeline, and understanding this before investing is critical.

- If a company is buying raw land (such as a cornfield for future development), the project may have a longer and riskier timeline due to zoning approvals, infrastructure development, and servicing requirements.

- If the project is an infill development (where construction is happening within an already established community), the timeline is shorter and lower risk, since the area is already serviced with hydro, water, and roads.

Real estate investing at this level requires trust. There are many people out there who will take investment money without ever finishing a project, leaving investors with nothing.

That's why doing your homework on the company, the team, and their past successes is just as important as analyzing the deal itself. If you're investing in development, you need to make sure you're working with people who deliver on their promises.

THE HARSH REALITY OF MARKET DISRUPTIONS

Investors need to understand that not every project goes exactly as planned. During the COVID-19 pandemic, the construction and development industry came to a complete halt for over two years.

- Supply chains were disrupted. Basic materials like lumber, steel, and concrete became impossible to secure.
- Labor shortages delayed projects as workers were unable to access sites.

- Inflation skyrocketed, making it impossible for developers to accurately predict costs.

Even well-structured projects were severely impacted. If an investor was expecting twenty-seven percent returns in four years, that timeline was now extended and they were just hoping to break even.

WHO SHOULD—AND SHOULDN'T—INVEST IN DEVELOPMENT PARTNERSHIPS

I work with passive investors every day. It's a huge part of my business. We raise hundreds of millions of dollars annually, whether through registered funds or cash investments.

Over time, I've learned an important lesson: Not everyone should invest in development projects. Some investors put every last dollar into high-return projects, hoping to make a big win. If something goes wrong, they're finished.

After everything that has happened in the industry, especially post-pandemic, it has become painfully clear that some people should never have put their money into development in the first place.

If you want a lower-risk option, a REIT investment is often the better choice. REITs provide:

- Diversified real estate ownership
- Cash flow from rental income

- Lower debt-to-equity ratios
- More liquidity than development partnerships

While they don't offer twenty-seven percent returns, they provide steady, stable, long-term growth, and you can redeem your investment if needed

For those who can afford to take on higher risk, development partnerships can be incredibly lucrative. For those who rely on their investment money for retirement or financial security, it's not always the right choice.

UNDERSTANDING THE STRUCTURE OF A DEVELOPMENT INVESTMENT

When we present an investment package, it's not just a simple proposal. It's a comprehensive, well-researched plan, put together by a team of specialists in different fields. Analysts, accountants, architects, engineers, developers, and construction managers—all working together to bring a project from concept to completion.

Speaking specifically about our company, here's how it works. The development team starts the process. We determine the current stage of approvals, how long it will take to secure zoning, site plan approvals, permits, and whether we're already at an advanced stage in the process, which can significantly reduce the timeline.

Then, we bring in the architects and engineers. They prepare schematic drawings, assessing how many units can fit on the property, the feasibility of underground parking, environmental considerations, and any potential concerns that need to be resolved before moving forward. This is followed by valuation reports, appraisals, and environmental assessments to ensure that the land and project are sound investments.

Once all of this information is compiled, the financial team steps in. They evaluate construction costs, financing structures, projected rental income, debt servicing, development charges, taxes, and other key expenses. All of these figures are compiled into a detailed investor package, which includes:

- A transparent breakdown of the deal
- Projected returns and timelines
- Market research and due diligence reports
- Legal, financial, and development team details
- Exit strategies (sale, rental, or refinancing options)

With this information, investors can make fully informed decisions, knowing exactly how their money is being deployed, who is managing the project, and what the expected outcomes are.

EVALUATING MARKET CONDITIONS AND RISK

In turbulent times, purpose-built rental housing is in extremely high demand due to the ongoing housing crisis. This makes it one of the best asset classes to invest in today.

On the other hand, a condo development in downtown Toronto, would not be something I'd pursue at this time. Five or ten years ago, condos in Toronto were the hottest investment opportunity, but today, with rising interest rates and market shifts, the risks are much higher.

LIMITED PARTNER VS. GENERAL PARTNER— WHO BEARS THE RISK?

One of the most important distinctions in a Limited Partnership (LP) structure is the difference between the Limited Partner and the General Partner.

- In a development project:
- I am the General Partner (GP). As the operator, I bear all the risk.

The investor is the Limited Partner (LP). They contribute capital but have no liability beyond their investment amount.

As the General Partner, I:

- Qualify for and guarantee the mortgages
- Handle all operations, payables, and financing obligations
- Take on the risk if the project faces challenges or financial difficulties

If something goes wrong, the Limited Partner has no liability for debts or financial obligations beyond their original investment.

Many investors love this structure because they don't have to qualify for a mortgage, and if additional funds are needed down the line, it's not their responsibility to provide more capital. Everything is clearly outlined in the partnership agreement, ensuring no unexpected cash calls for the Limited Partners.

HOW LIMITED PARTNERSHIP RETURNS WORK

A Limited Partnership investment is structured in different ways, depending on the deal. Typically:

- The Limited Partner (Investor) receives a minimum preferred return—for example, fifteen percent annually.
- Any profits above that threshold are split between the General Partner and Limited Partner— sometimes 50/50, sometimes 60/40, depending on the project's structure and potential returns.
  The size of the deal can vary. It could be:
- A triplex conversion
- A twelve-unit apartment development
- A multi-phase, large-scale development project

Regardless of the size, the Limited Partner's role remains the same, they invest capital while being shielded from liability and enjoying passive income and long-term appreciation.

KNOWING WHO YOU'RE INVESTING WITH

One of the most important factors in any real estate investment, whether it's a Limited Partnership, REIT, or development project, is knowing who you are investing with.

In a Limited Partnership structure, the company owns the property, and investors are issued shares or units in the project. If the General Partner or operators aren't trustworthy, lack experience, or fail to execute, investors could lose everything.

Here's what I've learned:

If an investor cannot afford to lose their investment in a worst-case scenario, then development projects and Limited Partnerships are not the right choice for them.

For those who need liquidity, a safer, more stable option like a REIT, where there is cash flow, diversification, and redemption flexibility, is a better choice.

For those who understand the risks and rewards of Limited Partnerships, these deals can be incredibly lucrative.

Know who you are investing with. Know the risks. Make sure you are working with people who have a proven track record of delivering on their promises.

PRIVATE MORTGAGES: A SECURE AND LUCRATIVE INVESTMENT

Private mortgages are a phenomenal investment vehicle for those looking for secured, passive income. While the returns are not as high as a limited partnership in real estate development, they offer stability, predictability, and asset-backed security.

A private mortgage is simply lending your money. Whether it's cash or registered funds (RRSPs, TFSAs, LIRAs, etc.) to another person who needs a mortgage. In return, your loan is secured against real estate.

This mortgage charge gives you a lien on the property, preventing the borrower from taking on additional financing in front of your mortgage without your approval. If they do, it's considered a breach of contract, which can put them into default.

HOW PRIVATE MORTGAGES WORK

Private mortgages are typically structured as interest-only loans, with a twelve-month term. The borrower has the option to:

- Prepay the full term upfront (some investors prefer this for guaranteed returns).
- Make monthly interest payments (either through post-dated checks or direct deposits).

At the end of the term, the mortgage broker will reach out to the lender to discuss renewal options. If the borrower needs to extend for another twelve months, they must:

- Pay a new lender fee (typically two percent).
- Provide updated financial documents (credit reports, tax statements, and proof of insurance).
- Show proof of ability to repay (ensuring the lender is still protected).

It is completely up to the lender whether they choose to extend the loan or request repayment at the end of the term.

WHY PRIVATE MORTGAGES ARE SO SECURE

One of the biggest advantages of private mortgages is that all funds go through a lawyer. The lawyer is responsible for:

- Registering the mortgage charge on title.
- Ensuring the title is clear (checking for any issues, such as tax arrears or undisclosed liens).
- Holding the funds in trust until all conditions are met.

Only when everything is legally secured and verified is the money released to the borrower's lawyer.

TYPICAL RETURNS ON PRIVATE MORTGAGES

The returns on private mortgages vary based on loan-to-value. (LTV)

- First mortgages typically earn eight to sixteen percent annually.
- The higher the loan-to-value ratio, the higher the interest rate.

Factors that affect interest rates and return levels include:

- The borrower's credit—Lower credit scores may require higher interest rates.
- Property location—Loans on properties in highly desirable areas have lower risk.
- Loan amount relative to value—A loan at fifty percent LTV is much safer than one at ninety percent LTV.
- Property type—Unique properties or land loans are riskier than standard residential homes.

If a borrower has challenged credit, owns a unique property, or is purchasing in a less desirable area, the loan will be considered riskier, and the lender will charge a higher interest rate to compensate.

WHO SHOULD INVEST IN
PRIVATE MORTGAGES?

Private mortgages are ideal for investors looking for steady, predictable cash flow without the responsibilities of owning and managing real estate. Unlike rental properties, there are no tenants, maintenance issues, or market fluctuations to worry about.

Investing in private mortgages through an experienced mortgage broker is critical. In Canada and the U.S., it is illegal to lend privately without using a licensed mortgage broker.

A professional broker:

- Connects lenders with qualified borrowers.
- Conducts all due diligence. (Credit analysis, property valuation, income verification).
- Ensures full legal compliance in all transactions.

WHY PRIVATE MORTGAGES WORK

Private mortgages are one of the safest and most lucrative passive investments, backed by real estate collateral. The lender bears minimal risk, as all funds are secured through legal contracts and registered mortgages.

PRIVATE LENDING AND SYNDICATED MORTGAGES

Private lending continues to be one of the best ways to generate passive income while securing your investment against real estate assets. Whether you are funding a single mortgage or participating in a syndicated mortgage, the key is understanding the structure, the security, and the process of enforcing the loan if things go wrong.

Let's say you are in small communities far from city centers, and you're lending on a small, rural property that needs significant repairs. The loan could be riskier and more expensive due to higher repair costs, fewer buyers in the market, and longer timeframes for refinancing or selling. This is where syndicated mortgages come into play.

WHAT IS A SYNDICATED MORTGAGE?

A syndicated mortgage allows multiple investors to pool their money together to fund a single mortgage loan.

For example, let's say a borrower needs $1 million in private second mortgage financing. The loan-to-value (LTV) of the real estate is reasonable at sixty percent, meaning the combined first and second mortgage debt equals only sixty percent of the property's value. If you only have $300,000 to invest, you can still participate.

We would bring in additional investors who contribute the remaining $700,000, and together, everyone shares in the returns from the mortgage interest payments. At thirteen to fourteen percent interest, this can be an excellent return, and because the loan is secured against real estate, it offers a strong level of protection.

WHAT HAPPENS IF THE BORROWER DEFAULTS?

If the borrower stops making payments, we follow a legal enforcement process to recover the funds.

1. Issue a Notice of Sale—The lender's lawyer sends a demand letter to the borrower, requiring payment.

2. File a Statement of Claim—If the borrower does not respond or refuses to pay, legal action is initiated, suing them personally and initiating a Power of Sale.

3. Borrower has thirty–thirty-six days to pay—The borrower must either pay the outstanding amount or the property is listed for sale.

4. The property is listed for at least sixty days—The lender cannot accept lowball offers immediately. The property must be fairly marketed to ensure maximum recovery.

5. Funds are distributed—Once the property is sold, the proceeds go toward covering outstanding mortgage payments, legal fees, broker fees, and other costs before the remaining funds are returned to the lender.

SECURITY IN PRIVATE LENDING

From an investor's standpoint, the security lies in the real estate itself. If the borrower defaults, the lender has the right to take legal action, sell the property, and recover the debt.

Today, private money is in high demand, and lenders can even use registered funds (RRSPs, TFSAs, LIRAs, etc.) to invest in private mortgages in Canada. However, each province has its own regulations. For example, in New Brunswick and Nova Scotia, we've had cases where the legal process is slower. Borrowers can delay foreclosure by claiming they have money coming in, sometimes dragging out the process for over a year.

WHY WORKING WITH THE RIGHT TEAM MATTERS

This is why it's critical to have an experienced mortgage broker and legal team handling the file. I take this very seriously—if someone defaults, I am all over them like a dirty shirt.

In our firm, we have never let our investors lose money. I treat every investor's money as if it's my own, because if there's a loss, I'm the one covering the shortfall.

THE END GOAL:
OWNING PAPER, NOT PROPERTY

For many real estate investors, the ultimate goal is to transition from owning physical properties to becoming a private lender. This allows them to sit back, collect interest payments, and enjoy passive income without the operational work.

Every month, interest payments roll in. At the end of the loan term, your original investment remains intact. You can then renew the mortgage, move your funds into a new deal, or cash out.

It's a low-maintenance way to earn strong returns, but it does require some active management:

- You need to track your investments and ensure payments are made on time.
- If a mortgage is paid out early, you must find a replacement deal to keep your money working.
- Most private mortgages last twelve to twenty-four months, so reinvesting is an ongoing process.

WHY PRIVATE LENDING WORKS

Private lending is one of the most profitable, secure, and passive ways to build wealth, if done correctly.

The key to success is:

1. Working with a trusted mortgage broker to connect with high-quality borrowers.

2. Structuring the loan properly, ensuring the loan-to-value ratio is reasonable.

3. Having a legal team in place to handle enforcement if necessary.

4. Understanding that private lending is short-term bridge financing, meaning your money will need to be reinvested periodically.

It's a smart, strategic way to build long-term wealth.

THE ROLE OF MORTGAGE ADMINISTRATORS IN PRIVATE LENDING

While private lending is one of the best passive income strategies, there is some management involved. However, for investors who travel frequently, live abroad, or simply don't want to deal with the administrative side of lending, using a mortgage administrator is a great solution. A mortgage administrator acts as a middleman, managing the entire lending process on your behalf.

- They register the mortgage in their name on title, but they do so on behalf of your interest. This adds a layer of privacy, as your personal or company name does not appear on title.

- They collect payments from the borrower, ensuring everything is paid on time.

- If a payment bounces (NSF), they chase it down and handle the communication.

- They manage renewals, coordinating with the borrower and ensuring the mortgage continues or is paid out.
- If the borrower defaults, the administrator steps in, handling the legal enforcement process on your behalf.

All of this is done for a one percent fee on the loan amount, which is a small price to pay for the peace of mind that everything is handled professionally. For many investors, this is the best way to lend privately without any hands-on involvement. You don't have to worry about collecting payments, chasing down defaults, or managing renewals.

RANKING PASSIVE INVESTMENT STRATEGIES BY RISK

If we were to rank real estate investment vehicles by risk, from least risky to most risky, it would look something like this:

1. REITs (Real Estate Investment Trusts)—Lowest risk, fully managed, diversified real estate holdings.
2. Private Mortgages—Moderate risk, secured against real estate with legal recourse in case of default.
3. Limited Partnerships—Higher risk, as funds are tied to development projects with longer timelines and potential market fluctuations.

Many of my long-term clients have built incredible wealth strictly through real estate investing. Some started as real estate owners, built up portfolios, and later transitioned into private lending through family trusts. Others are doctors, professionals, or retirees who wanted passive cash flow without the headaches of property management.

USING THE BANK'S MONEY TO EARN HIGHER RETURNS

A smart strategy for investors, especially those in retirement, is using the bank's money to fund their lending investments.

For example, my own mother is a private lender. I got a mortgage on her house, borrowing money at five–six percent interest and lending it out at fifteen percent interest, making the spread between the two rates.

This is a brilliant way to leverage capital, you borrow at a low rate and reinvest at a much higher return. The only difference is that mortgage interest is tax-deductible, while private lending income is taxed as regular income.

TAX CONSIDERATIONS FOR DIFFERENT INVESTMENT TYPES

- Private mortgage lending—Returns are taxed as income, meaning they are taxed at the highest bracket.

- Limited Partnerships—Typically taxed as capital gains, which is more tax-efficient.
- REITs—Gains from a REIT are also considered capital gains, unless they are held in registered accounts like RRSPs or TFSAs, in which case they are tax-free or tax-deferred.

PASSIVE INVESTING THE SMART WAY

For investors looking for hands-off real estate investing, REITs, private mortgages, and limited partnerships all provide different levels of risk and return.

- REITs are the most stable and work well for those who want diversification, liquidity, and long-term appreciation.
- Private mortgages provide strong, fixed income, secured by real estate assets, making them a great choice for retirees or those looking for monthly cash flow.
- Limited partnerships offer the highest return potential, but they come with higher risks and longer investment timelines.

Ultimately, the best investment strategy depends on the individual investor's goals, risk tolerance, and need for liquidity.

18

FEEL THE DEAL

For me, it has always been about feeling the deal. I can look at a real estate package in two minutes and immediately get a sense of whether it's good or bad. That's not because of some formula or checklist. It's because I've nurtured that intuition for so long.

Intuition isn't something you're just born with, it's something you develop. It takes time, experience, and yes, failure. Too often, people ignore the feeling of a deal. They look at numbers, at spreadsheets, at surface-level analysis, but they don't stop to ask themselves if it feels right.

If you're building your real estate business, you will have successes, but you will also have failures. The failures will teach you more than the wins ever will.

The real question isn't how do I avoid failure? You can't. The real question is how do you accept failure? How do you use it to grow? How do you take the lessons from your mistakes and apply them to your next opportunity?

Even today, I face challenges. The difference is, I don't look at them as negatives. Instead, I ask myself why this is happening, what the lesson is, what I did wrong, and what I would do differently next time?

If there's one mistake I've made repeatedly, it's jumping into too many things at once. My mind is always bursting with ideas. I want to do everything right away, and sometimes, I stretch myself too thin.

Will I still make mistakes? Of course. We all will, until the day we die. The real key is to pick up the pieces, absorb the lessons, and use them to navigate the next step. Sometimes the next step is completely different from what you expected. Other times, it's just a better version of the same plan, but executed with more wisdom and experience.

There are times when life feels like it's hitting you from every direction at once. It's overwhelming. It's exhausting. It's easy to get lost in it, to doubt yourself, to feel like you're drowning in negativity. When you're in that space, there's only one way out. Step back. Slow down. Look around. The answers are already inside you. It's during the hardest moments that your inner voice becomes clearest, if you are willing to listen to it.

Most people don't listen. They get so caught up in the chaos that they ignore their gut, ignore the signs, ignore the feeling that's been guiding them all along. If you slow down and tune in, you will feel the direction you need to take.

Everyone has a different perspective on life, and I don't judge that. For some it's is the universe, for me, I believe that everything happens according to God's will, His guidance and direction. Maybe for you, it's faith. Maybe it's just your own instincts, built over years of experience. Whatever it is, trust it.

The next time a big decision comes your way, don't just look at the numbers. Don't just listen to the experts. Feel the deal. Ask yourself if this feels right, if you see the opportunity clearly, and if you're listening to your gut. Your next success is already waiting for you. You just need to listen, and go after it.

MASTERING THE MARKET CYCLES: TRUSTING YOUR INTUITION IN REAL ESTATE

Positivity will help you a lot when things are down. This is when you need to rely on your intuition to make moves, rather than getting caught up in fear or following what everyone else is doing.

I don't believe in following the herd. It's not about what the majority is doing. It's about what feels right. You have to filter out the negative energy, whether it's coming from the media, from people around you, or from the general sentiment in the market. The best opportunities are rarely found by doing what everyone else is doing.

If you are in a strong financial position, the worst thing you can do is sit on the sidelines because of fear. When markets are down, that is when the best deals appear. That is when you should be looking for opportunities that others are too scared to go after.

I have a client I will never forget. He was an older gentleman who started buying properties in the 1980s and 90s, during one of the worst real estate crashes. Everyone around him was panicking, trying to sell their properties, convinced that real estate was a terrible investment. He saw something different. He told me how builders and developers were desperate to sell, offering no-money-down deals to get people to buy. He took full advantage of those deals, acquiring multiple properties with none of his own money. His friends ridiculed him, calling him crazy. They told him he would lose everything.

He didn't listen. He kept going. Years later, he had millions and millions of dollars in equity. Those properties he bought when the market was down became a massive empire. He went from having nothing to being a multi-millionaire, all because he saw opportunity when others only saw fear. That is the difference between investors who build real wealth and those who get stuck in short-term fear-based thinking.

If you've been building your real estate business, by this point, you should have the confidence to do the same.

Even if you're a new investor, this is an opportunity. Challenged markets create the best opportunities.

When interest rates are high, when inflation is up, when there is a recession and people are afraid. This is when you should be buying real estate.

People hold onto their money in times of uncertainty, gripping it tightly, convinced that the worst is coming. That is exactly when investors should be stepping in and making smart, calculated moves.

If I were sitting on cash right now, I would be buying as many properties as I could. Of course, it has to be a calculated purchase. You don't just rush in and buy without doing your due diligence.

Real estate is like the stock market, it goes up and down, but over the long term, it always goes up. It's rare to see a market downturn that lasts indefinitely. Land is finite. As the population grows and immigration increases, acquiring property will only become more difficult and more expensive.

Opportunities don't last forever. Those who see beyond the fear and make informed, confident decisions will be the ones who succeed in the long run. You still do your due diligence on each property. Everything that's been covered in this book—the fundamentals of analyzing a deal, ensuring structural integrity, verifying financials, and assessing market conditions, all of it still applies.

You're not looking to buy a money pit or take on unnecessary risk just because the market is down. The key difference in challenging market conditions is that everyone else is afraid. That fear stops people from seeing opportunities clearly and taking action when they should. Fear is powerful. It cripples people's ability to move forward.

I'm not saying to put every last penny into real estate. That would be reckless. If you have the capacity, if you have the financial ability, then this is the time to act. Even if it's a small cottage, a single rental unit, or an entry-level home, just getting into real estate during a downturn puts you in a strong position for the rebound.

When the market comes back, those who bought when things were uncertain will find themselves holding assets that have dramatically increased in value. Those who let fear keep them on the sidelines will be the ones struggling to get in.

When market fear spreads, it's thick, like a fog you can feel in the air. It clouds judgment, kills momentum, and makes people second-guess themselves. That's why you have to connect with your inner Feel the Deal instinct.

Step back from the negativity, look at the investment with a clear head, and ask yourself:

Does this make sense?

Can I break even or generate cash flow?

Is there enough cushion in my numbers to absorb market fluctuations?

Interest rates fluctuate, and if you're planning for long-term success, your numbers have to be realistic. Don't run your calculations at two or three percent. Those days may never come back. Use six percent as a benchmark, or even ten percent if you want to be conservative. If the deal still works at those numbers, it's a strong investment.

When times are tough, sellers are motivated, and this is when creativity in real estate financing truly comes into play. Sellers may allow you to assume their mortgages at low interest rates. They may hold a second mortgage for you. You might find no-money-down deals that wouldn't be possible in a booming market.

Yes, some people will be in dire financial situations, which is unfortunate, but it is the reality of market cycles. For those who are positioned well, this is when the best deals appear, opportunities that can change the trajectory of your wealth for years to come.

THE REAL ESTATE CYCLE: FROM INVESTOR TO PASSIVE INCOME

No matter what your real estate strategy is, whether you own Airbnb vacation rentals, multifamily apartment buildings, or you're a builder and developer, the opportunities never stop. In uncertain markets, properties are selling for thirty cents on the dollar, which means there are excellent investment opportunities for those who are ready to act.

When the market is strong, there are still deals. You may be at a point where it's time to sell properties and capitalize on appreciation, or maybe you have long-term holds that will stay in your family trust for generations.

Multifamily investments, in particular, have always been recession-proof. People will always need a place to live. Even when the economy slows down, people still rent, which is why multifamily is one of the safest asset classes. Banks continue to finance rental buildings even in challenging times because the demand for housing never disappears.

THE TRANSITION FROM ACTIVE INVESTOR TO PASSIVE LENDER

Many investors, after years of growing their portfolio, eventually transition away from being landlords. Even with property managers handling day-to-day operations, being an owner still comes with responsibilities.

At some point, many investors decide to sell and shift their capital into passive mortgage lending, they move from owning real estate to owning paper. That's the point when financial freedom becomes real.

I'll continue building amazing properties all over the world, expanding Once Upon a Stay, creating beautiful real estate experiences, but I also want to travel, enjoy life, and have complete financial independence.

If you're at the stage where you are liquidating assets, selling properties that you no longer want to manage, and walking away with significant cash flow, the smartest move is to invest that capital into mortgage lending.

Let's say you've built a portfolio over ten to twenty years. You've accumulated significant equity, and now the market is primed for selling. You sell five or ten properties and end up with $10 million in cash. Instead of reinvesting in more properties, you take that $10 million and become a lender. Regardless of whether it's a strong or weak real estate market, you are earning twelve–fourteen percent annually on your capital.

THE GENERATIONAL WEALTH MINDSET

Many lenders I know started as first-generation investors. They built their wealth through real estate investing, then transitioned into mortgage lending, and eventually passed their lending businesses on to their children, creating multi-generational wealth.

This is the real estate cycle, starting small, growing, building equity, and scaling until you reach a point where your money makes money for you. Some people will always stay active in real estate, continuing to buy, sell, and develop for decades.

It's about reaching a place where you don't have to work unless you want to, where your investments are providing for your lifestyle, and where your mind is mentally free from financial stress. That's the power of building wealth strategically and knowing when to transition from active investor to passive investor.

RETHINKING THE MORTGAGE PAYOFF MENTALITY

Most people are made to believe that paying off your mortgage as soon as possible is the smartest financial move. I've never been a pay-off-your-mortgage person. Why? I know how to leverage money.

Even if you're paying seven or even ten percent interest on a mortgage, you can borrow that money and lend it out at fifteen or twenty percent. You're still making money on the spread.

To me, the idea of a free-and-clear house with dead equity just sitting there not performing for you is crazy. Your home or investment property should be working for you.

This is where private lending becomes a key part of the equation. It should be something investors integrate into their journey early on, even in small amounts, so that they learn how it works, get comfortable with it, and build it into their long-term financial strategy.

KEEPING INVESTMENTS PRIVATE AND HANDS-OFF

If you work with a mortgage administrator, for example, our company Pro Funds, your information stays private and everything is managed for you. You don't have to spend time chasing payments, following up on loans, or handling the paperwork. You can keep running your business, managing your family, or focusing on other priorities while still having money working for you behind the scenes.

WHY THE "OLD WORLD" MENTALITY HOLDS PEOPLE BACK

For generations, people have been told the same thing: work hard, pay off your mortgage, pay off all your bills, save money, and invest in RRSPs.

This outdated thinking is not how wealth is built. I see it all the time, immigrants come to the country, work incredibly hard, and put every penny toward paying off their house. They sacrifice for years, living frugally, making extra payments, determined to own their home outright.

What happens when they finally do? They have a fully paid-off house, yes, but zero passive income. They are now sitting on dead equity.

HOW TO USE HOME EQUITY TO GENERATE PASSIVE INCOME

Instead of just sitting on a paid-off house, why not leverage that equity to make money? Say you own a house worth $1 million and it's fully paid off. Instead of just letting that $1 million sit there, you refinance the property and take out $500,000 as a mortgage. You set up the mortgage on a twenty-five year amortization at seven percent interest. The longer the amortization, the lower the payments, which makes cash flow easier to manage.

Now, take that $500,000 and invest it in private mortgages, specifically first mortgages, which are low-risk. A conservative return on a first mortgage investment is fourteen percent. Now you're earning fourteen percent on that $500,000, while your mortgage costs are only seven percent. The spread between those two rates is seven percent, which means you're making money off borrowed money, just like the banks do.

For people who don't or can't work, maybe seniors or those who aren't in a position to earn active income, sitting on a paid-off home is a lost opportunity. They could be accessing that home equity and turning it into income through private mortgage investments.

This strategy changed my mother's life. After my father passed away, she was left with a small mortgage. We refinanced her property, took out as much as we could, and invested it in mortgage lending. She was able to pay her mortgage every month from the returns while still pocketing an extra $3,000 to $4,000 a month in net cash flow. That decision gave her financial freedom. She could actually live, travel, and do things she never thought she could afford.

This is why I believe in using the bank's money wisely instead of rushing to pay everything off. It's not about debt, it's about leverage. It's about making your assets work for you.

LEVERAGING HOME EQUITY FOR PASSIVE INCOME AND FINANCIAL FREEDOM

People can take advantage of the equity in their home, whether it's $100,000, $500,000, or even $1 million. The same financial principles apply no matter the amount.

If you own a $1 million home and your mortgage balance is only fifty percent of the value, you can go to the bank and refinance up to 80 percent loan-to-value. After paying off your existing mortgage, the remaining funds are available as capital you can invest.

Some people prefer to use a home equity line of credit (HELOC) instead of refinancing. This approach allows flexibility, as you only pay interest on the amount you use, and as the money comes in from investments, it can be used to pay down the line of credit.

For a real estate investor, a HELOC can limit borrowing power for new property purchases because banks count the full credit limit as potential debt, even if you haven't used it. If you plan to invest in real estate, a traditional mortgage refinance is often the better choice because the funds are set, and the debt-to-income ratio impact is lower.

For someone strictly using the funds for private lending, however, a line of credit works well. Since it's interest-only, it keeps monthly costs low, while allowing you to earn significantly higher returns through private mortgage investments.

This strategy allows people to live off their investments while still owning their home, rather than simply focusing on paying off the mortgage as fast as possible. The equity in a home is an asset.

HOW THIS STRATEGY HAS CHANGED LIVES

Over the years, we have helped so many people unlock the potential of their home equity to improve their financial situation.

For some, it was creating an extra income stream while still working. For others, it helped support aging parents, covering the costs of long-term care facilities. It provided a financial cushion without forcing them to dip into their primary income or savings.

Eventually, as real estate investments grow and mature, the goal is to sell off part of the portfolio and transition into full-time lending in retirement. This is not something that's widely taught, because the system doesn't want you to know about it. They want you to follow the standard rules, to pay off your house, work your job, save money in low-yield investments, and stay in the system. There are better ways to build wealth.

UNDERSTANDING RISK AND SMART INVESTING

No investment is 100 percent risk-free. A borrower could default, and as an investor, you need to have a financial cushion to absorb potential delays or legal proceedings.

The people who follow the principles in this book, who trust their intuition and develop their Feel the Deal instincts, will understand how to make creative, smart investments.

This is a brilliant way to build passive income, but like anything in real estate, it requires strategy and discipline. Even if you start small, by securing a home equity line of credit and using it to fund private mortgages, you can begin growing your passive income stream.

KEY SUCCESS PRINCIPLES

There are a few key principles that I believe are essential to real estate success.

Win-Win Deals: Every investment should be structured so that everyone benefits. The borrower gets the funds they need, the lender earns a strong return, and all parties involved walk away happy. A true win-win deal ensures fairness and long-term success.

Honesty: Creativity in real estate is critical, but so is integrity. You can be innovative, flexible, and strategic, but never compromise on honesty. The best investors build their businesses on trust and transparency, which is why they continue to grow and succeed.

Real estate is about opportunity, creativity, and calculated risk-taking. Those who learn to leverage their assets wisely, invest strategically, and think beyond traditional methods will achieve true financial freedom.

GET BACK UP

Don't let things keep you down. Wipe off the dirt, get back up, and keep going. Sometimes, it takes time to get there because mentally, you need to heal from the wounds. Once you do, you go back stronger and wiser.

Every setback teaches you something. Every fall gives you a lesson. Those lessons, over time, shape your success.

POSITIVITY

You need to be positive. Manifesting positive energy and thinking positively is real. You have to believe with conviction.

Tell yourself, *this will happen*. Say it over and over again. No matter how clouded your mind gets, push the negativity out. Get rid of the doubt. Just say, *Nope, this is going to happen. This is going to happen.*

FOLLOW YOUR GUT

If you're looking to buy something or make an investment, you have to feel the deal. If something doesn't feel right, even if everyone is pressuring you to do it, walk away. It doesn't matter how good it looks on paper. If your gut is telling you something is off, listen to it.

Now, if you're the type of person who questions everything and is crippled by fear, you need to dig deeper to figure out whether it's just your anxiety talking. If an opportunity keeps throwing challenges at you, if it feels like the universe is blocking it at every turn, it's not the right one. There will always be another deal. Often, the next one is better than the one you walked away from.

FEAR

Fear can cripple you in business. You have to step outside your comfort zone, but you don't have to dive in blindly. You don't have to drown and get back up, then drown again.

Don't be reactive. Take your time. Make sure your decisions are smart and well-calculated. You should feel the deal, but you also need to make sure the numbers make sense.

Be smart. Be wise. Think before you act.

LISTEN TO YOUR ELDERS

They are wise. They have lived through it all. If you ever get a chance to sit in a room with an older person who has been in the business for decades, pay attention. An eighty year-old who has spent a lifetime in real estate or business has far more wisdom than someone in their thirties or forties. They've seen cycles, they've watched markets shift, and they've navigated challenges that younger investors haven't yet experienced.

STAY FOCUSED

This has been my biggest personal struggle, staying focused. I take on too much at once, and that has been one of my hardest lessons. Success isn't about doing everything. It's about doing a few things exceptionally well.

If you focus on one, two, or three things and give them 100,000 percent of your energy, you will succeed. If you let other people's advice, distractions, and outside noise pull you in different directions, you'll lose momentum.

In my life, everything has come in phases. I started with single-family homes, then moved into multifamily, then into development, and then into construction.

When you take on a project, do it well. Put everything you have into it. When you put out that kind of energy, success follows.

THE END—FOR NOW

This is my first book, but it won't be my last.

There are still so many stories to tell, lessons to share, and experiences ahead. Real estate is an endless journey, and as I continue to grow, build, and expand, there will be more books filled with even bigger deals, greater risks, and even greater rewards.

My goal is to expand our enterprise across North America and ultimately take the company public. That chapter of the journey will be another book, one that will document the process of scaling, structuring, and executing a vision on a whole new level.

Beyond that, I have a dream. One day, I will buy castles in Europe and transform them into legendary vacation destinations. I don't mean ordinary hotels or resorts, I'm talking about off-the-charts, once-in-a-lifetime, breathtaking experiences that will bring people from all over the world to see, stay, and live in some of the most unique, historic, and incredible properties ever imagined.

I can already picture it, digging through ancient buildings, uncovering hidden treasures buried in history, restoring centuries-old architecture, and breathing life back into places filled with stories and mystery.

This is my passion. This is my dream. Like everything else in my life, I will make it happen.

This is not the end. It's just the beginning.